NCE Exam
Prep
2023-2024

Study Guide with 410 Practice
Questions and Answer
Explanations for the National
Counselor Examination

Contents

Introduction 1

Chapter One: What to Expect 4
    Content Outline 4
    Registration 11
    Scheduling 13
    Taking the Exam 14
    Following The Exam 19

Chapter Two: Preparing for the Exam **21**
    Study Guide 21
    Studying for the NCE 25

Chapter Three: Professional Orientation and Ethical Practice **28**
    Counseling Defined 28
    Historical Overview 28
    CACREP Standards 31
    Other Current And Continuing Trends 33
    ACA Advocacy Competencies 34
    Profession 39
    The CACREP 41
    Certification 42
    The NBCC 42
    Licensure 43
    Confidentiality and Privileged Communication 44
    Duty to Warn 44

Duty to Protect 45
Other Important Terms 45
Code of Ethics 48
Questions and Answers 49
Answer Key 54

Chapter Four: Social and Cultural Diversity 55
List Of Terms 55
Questions and Answers 64
Answer Key 69

Chapter Five: Human Growth and Development 70
Foundational Issues 70
Special designs in HGD research 71
The central nervous system (CNS) 72
The brain 73
Genetic disorders 74
Classical conditioning 75
Operant conditioning 76
Social learning 76
The Dollard and Miller approach 76
Cognitive development 77
Lev Vygotsky's cognitive development theory 77
Cognition and memory 78
Other important concepts in cognitive development 78
Personality development 79
Questions and Answers 81
Answer Key 86

Chapter Six: Career Development 87
Important Terms 87
Questions and Answers 93
Answer Key 98

Chapter Seven: Counseling and Helping Relationships 99
Important Topics 99
Questions and Answers 107
Answer Key 112

Chapter Eight: Group Counseling and Group Work **113**
Important points 113
Questions and Answers 116
Answer Key 121

Chapter Nine: Assessment and Testing **122**
Important Points 122
Questions and Answers 127
Answer Key 132

Chapter Ten: Research and Program Evaluation **133**
Important Points 133
Questions and Answers 135
Answer Key 140

Chapter Eleven: Full-Length Exam **141**
Answer Key 177
Answers And Explanations 179
Bonus Fifty 191
Answer Key 202

Conclusion **204**

References **206**
Additional Quizlets and Factsheets for Information 211

Free Video Offer!

Thank you for purchasing from Hanley Test Preparation! We're honored to help you prepare for your exam. To show our appreciation, we're offering an Exclusive Test Tips Video.

This video includes multiple strategies that will make you successful on your big exam.

All we ask is that you email us your feedback and describe your experience with our product. Amazing, awful, or just so-so. We want to hear what you have to say!

To get your FREE VIDEO, just send us an email at bonusvideo@hanleytestprep.com with **Free Video** in the subject line and the following information in the body of the email:

- The name of the product you purchased
- Your product rating on a scale of 1-5, with 5 being the highest rating.
- Your feedback about the product.

If you have any questions or concerns, please don't hesitate to contact us at support@hanleytestprep.com

Thanks again!

Introduction

About ten years ago, I began a journey to help professional counselors ace the National Counselor Exam. Among other reasons, I realized that the world will always need certified professionals to show them sustainable ways to exist.

It all starts with the National Board for Certified Counselors, Inc. and Affiliates (NBCC).

The NBCC develops and administers national certification and state licensure exams for professionals. These assess the skills and knowledge needed for counselors to practice efficiently, competently, and within the limits of professional ethics. Its purpose is to protect the general public by ensuring the ones who counsel them are qualified and competent enough to do so. The NBCC boasts over 66,000 certified counselors across the United States and over 40 countries. Its examinations are used by all 50 states, Puerto Rico, and the District of Columbia as a means of accrediting counselors.

Among other examinations, the National Counselor Examination (NCE) is administered by the NBCC. Its purpose is to assess entry-level counselors, and it is a prerequisite certification for many state licensing boards. It is one of the two National Certified Counselor (NCC) certification examination options. Many military health systems also accept it as a means to identify recognized care providers.

From January 1st to December 31st, 2022, 3,548 NCEs have been administered. Of these, 2,794 candidates took the exam for the first time. They had a pass rate of 83.4%. Overall, 2,711 counselors were certified in 2022 (Initial Certification | *NBCRNA* 2023).

Some of us in counseling aim to pass the NCE because it's the primary requirement for obtaining professional counselor licensure in many parts of the U.S. In addition, passing the NCE serves as a competency hallmark. The NBCC is a well-respected organization in the counseling profession. Those who pass the NCE automatically get the same stamp of respect by demonstrating they have what it takes to become efficient and ethical counselors. Finally, the NCE comes with a host of career benefits. It is a way to show employers and clients that a counselor has met and aced rigorous professional standards, is well-versed in the field, and is highly competent.

Passing the NCE also brings you closer to a community of individuals who have gone through the wringer the same way as you. You get to interact with like-minded people and build a meaningful professional community. You also become someone who has the mark of a "professional who knows their field—" which means that others look up to you as a mentor.

So, with so many counselors vying for the golden pass mark, what are the issues regarding doing well in the exam?

Firstly, the NCE encapsulates a whole world of topics. Knowing where to begin and how to prioritize time and resources can be very challenging. Then there's the entire issue of memorizing multiple theories and concepts. Readers are often plagued by the fear of forgetting essential points while under pressure to perform. We also don't want to lose our heads when the exam draws closer because this means we obsess over questions we're not sure about and time that's flying away.

We also need to remember this is a mental game. Too many of us get lost in the nitty-gritty of personal anxiety and self-doubt, and we think we're too inadequate or don't have what it takes to make the cut. The reality is usually more straightforward.

I've been in your shoes. It's great to want to become successful, sought-after counselors. This means you take your profession and passions seriously. If you've found your way to this guidebook, you want to enhance your professional and personal growth, achieve success, and help the world. You aspire to become your role models— established professionals who have become trailblazers in the field. And you know that one of the fundamental steps to getting there is passing the NCE.

You're in the right place. Through this comprehensive, compact guidebook, you and I will review all the essentials needed to clear the NCE and begin your journey as an accredited professional counselor. I've packed this book with study materials and practice tests to help you. The practice tests will mimic the actual exam's patterns, and the content in each chapter will equip you with the information and the confidence you need to do well in these tests and the main one.

Are you ready to begin the process of becoming the next NCE-certified counselor? Let's begin!

Chapter One: What to Expect

In this chapter, we will cover everything you can expect from the examination.

The NCE's primary purpose is to assess the overall capability of examinees looking to become certified counselors at the entry-level. It measures their theoretical and skill-based knowledge to evaluate whether they have what is necessary to help society heal competently and safely.

The target population for the exam comprises entry-level counselors who have received appropriate education in counseling as per the minimum qualification requirements.

Content Outline

The NCE covers 200 multiple-choice questions (MCQs). Of these, 160 are scored, while 40 are not. The 40 unscored MCQs can be used for various reasons, including pre-testing novel questions or gathering feedback and information on the examinee's experience.

Unscored questions could assess demography (e.g., ethnicity, age, gender), the test-taker's opinions, or facilitate further research and evaluation. Scored and unscored questions follow the same layout and exist in jumbled order. As a test-taker, you have three hours and 45 minutes to finish the exam.

The exam contains questions reflecting topics from the original eight CACREP content areas. There are also questions from six work behaviors determined by a national job analysis of over 16,000 certified counselors. Each of these six domains test specific knowledge, skills, and tasks. These six are:

1. Professional Practice and Ethics. The knowledge, skills, and tasks for this ensure you, as the counselor, maintain clinical and administrative protocols and assess your ability to:

    o   Work with different clients based on their specific needs.
    o   Comprehend statistical methods and concepts relevant to research.
    o   Follow ethical and legal tenets while practicing.
    o   Set clear counselor and client roles.
    o   Delineate different rights and responsibilities of each client.
    o   Set confidentiality limits.
    o   Lay down counselor agency protocols, procedures, and policies.
    o   Discuss and review fees and insurance benefits.
    o   Elaborate and explain the relevant counseling processes, procedures for each, and associated risks and rewards.
    o   Explain the use and limitations of social media.
    o   Provide clear information about legal aspects.
    o   Procure informed consent.
    o   Discuss confidentiality about electronic communication.

2. Intake, Assessment, and Diagnosis. This section covers the counselors' knowledge, skills, and abilities (KSA) to conduct client absorption, assessment, and diagnosis. Sub-topics covered include your ability to:

    o   Conduct biopsychosocial interviews.
    o   Conduct diagnostic interviews.
    o   Carry out cultural formulation interviews.
    o   Execute initial interviews.
    o   Accurately determine diagnosis.
    o   Perform necessary mental status exams (MSE).
    o   Look into the possibility of co-occurring diagnoses.
    o   Determine the levels of care required.
    o   Determine the requisite treatment modality.

- o Assess presenting problems and distress levels.
- o Evaluate the mental health functioning of concerned individuals.
- o Screen clients to provide needed services.
- o Choose, employ, and study the instruments for assessment.
- o Employ formal and informal methods of observation.
- o Assess trauma and substance use possibilities.
- o Obtain self-reports from clients.
- o Evaluate dynamics of interaction.
- o Conduct ongoing assessments for at-risk behaviors, including homicide, injury to self or others, and suicide.
- o Use pre and post-test measures for assessing outcomes.
- o Evaluate the effectiveness of counseling procedures.

3. Areas of Clinical Focus. This is all about the counselors' ability, skills, and knowledge related to different areas of client concerns, including:

- o Any adjustments necessitated by physical injuries, losses, and medical conditions
- o Concerns about age and old-age issues
- o Behavioral issues
- o Bullying
- o Issues related to caregiving
- o Cultural adjustments
- o End-of-life decision-making issues
- o Panic and fear arising
- o Financial concerns
- o Gender identity issues
- o Grief and loss
- o Depression and hopelessness
- o Attachment issues and loneliness
- o Hyper or hypo mental focus
- o Issues about intellectual functioning
- o Problem sleeping or insomnia
- o Disruptive eating behaviors
- o Issues related to remarriage and recommitment
- o Developmental tasks
- o Obsessive behavioral thoughts

o Physical effects of anxiety
o Physical impacts of depression
o Issues stemming from trauma
o Addiction to harmful processes like gambling
o Racism and other forms of oppression
o Conflict on religious values
o Fear surrounding retirement
o Intrusive thoughts and rumination
o Dissociation from primary guardians
o Issues related to sexual function
o Sleeping patterns
o Existential concerns
o Stress and its management
o Addiction issues
o Suicidal thought patterns
o Terminal illness concerns
o Hallucinations (visual/auditory)
o Anxiety and worry
o Adoption concerns
o Blended family concerns
o Child abuse issues
o Child development concerns
o Problems related to dating and relationships
o Divorce Concerns
o Issues surrounding family abuse and violence
o Interpersonal concerns regarding violence from partners
o Communication problems
o Parenting and co-parenting tensions
o Emotional dysregulation

4. Treatment Planning: This concerns the counselors' capabilities in developing a practical treatment course. The concerns include:

o Collaborating with clients to establish objectives and goals relevant to the treatment.
o Establishing short and long goals in tandem with client diagnoses.
o Identifying barriers that could prevent clients from attaining their goals.

- o Identifying strengths that could improve the chance to attain goals.
- o Referring to different treatment levels like outpatient, residential, inpatient, and so on.
- o Referring to others regarding concurrent treatment.
- o Guiding treatment planning.
- o Discussing termination procedures and related issues.
- o Discussing group membership transitions.
- o Following up with patients after discharge.
- o Using assessment instrument outcomes for proper decision-making related to the client(s).
- o Reviewing and revising treatment plans.
- o Engaging clients in progress reviews toward their goals.
- o Collaborating with support systems and other providers for purposes like report writing and documentation.
- o Discussing integration and maintenance of progress in therapy.
- o Educating the client about the value of complying with treatment plans.

5. Counseling Skills and Interventions. This is all about the counselors' ability to work effectively. The pointers include:

- o Aligning intervention with the developmental levels of clients.
- o Aligning intervention with modalities of counseling— for example, if the counseling involves a single person, a couple, a group, a family, etc.
- o Aligning intervention with the demography— that is, if the clients are minorities, veterans, disabled, and so forth.
- o Implementing individual counseling related to treatment plans.
- o Applying counseling interventions that are in tune with relevant theory.
- o Addressing addiction problems.
- o Addressing cultural factors.
- o Addressing family compositions.
- o Evaluating and explaining interaction patterns.
- o Exploring interactions between family members.
- o Exploring values related to religions and spirituality.
- o Guiding clients in skill or strategy development to help them deal with their issues.
- o Assisting clients to build support systems.
- o Helping clients get motivated about making progressive changes.

o Improving interaction patterns.

o Providing crisis interventions.

o Educating clients about defense mechanisms and transference issues (where they may be unconditionally projecting their thoughts and feelings onto someone else).

o Facilitating relationships based on trust.

o Building communication skills.

o Developing strategies related to resolving conflicts.

o Developing safety plans.

o Facilitating systematic changes.

o Providing long-distance counseling.

o Providing educational resources that can facilitate stress management, adjustment to life changes like divorce or the loss of a loved one, and so on.

o Providing psychoeducation to clients.

o Summarize.

o Reframe and redirect.

o Facilitate empathic conversations.

o Employ self-disclosure.

o Employ constructive confrontation procedures.

o Generate awareness of in-the-moment interactions.

o Facilitate interpersonal conflict resolution.

o Facilitate group-specific linking and blocking. Linking helps make connections between different emotions, thoughts, and experiences. Blocking, in contrast, is suppressing and avoiding thoughts, emotions, and experiences.

o Manage leader and member dynamics.

o Be receptive to feedback.

o Address the impact of extended families.

o Contain and address intense or complex feelings.

o Explore the influence of patterns emerging from origin families.

o Address social support network impacts.

o Employ structured activities. These are planned, organized activities people partake in depending on their social roles or the parts they play in groups and organizations. They could be roles related to religious activities, community service projects, and so on.

o Encourage interactions among different group members.

  o Promote interactions between members and group leaders.
  o Employ psychoeducation as part of different group processes.
  o Elucidation group process phases.
  o Identify patterns and themes in groups.
  o Build interventions based on the levels of development in groups.
  o Challenge non-conducive harmful behaviors in groups.
  o Address possible interaction between out-of-group members.

6. Core Counseling Attributes. This covers effective counselors' traits, behaviors, and core behavioral patterns. It includes:

  o Self-awareness and knowledge of the impact of the self on clients
  o Integrity
  o Harmony and Compatibility
  o Sensitivity to issues surrounding gender, including gender orientation
  o Sensitivity and awareness of multicultural issues
  o Ability to tolerate and resolve conflicts
  o Empathic congruence
  o Ability to respond with empathy
  o Ability to successfully implement therapy in context to groups
  o Neutrality
  o Positivity
  o Respect for diversity
  o Ability to listen, be attentive, and reflect on client's concerns

These empirically validated work behaviors are considered most relevant to ensure that the counselor is a proficient practitioner. The content validity rests on these six and the eight content areas determined by CACREP. These areas are the common core areas and should be the central focus of your studying. They include:

1. Professional counseling orientation and ethical practice, spanning different aspects of professional functioning. This includes professional standards and ethics, roles, history, organizational structures, and credential procedures.
2. Social and cultural diversity, covering trends and topics that form the cornerstone of diverse, multicultural societies.

3. Human development and growth, including a comprehensive under-standing of the needs and traits of human beings at different develop-mental levels.
4. Career development.
5. Counseling and helping relationships, extending over different counsel-ing and consultation procedures.
6. Group work and group counseling, providing an understanding of group dynamics and counseling methods, theories, and other group work methods.
7. Assessment and testing, covering individual and group approach to both.
8. Research and program evaluation, encircling types of research methods and the ethical and legal considerations therein, along with basic statistics.

Now that we know what the structural foundation of the NCE covers, the next natural question is— how do we register for it, and how do we determine our eligibility? Let's go into this.

Registration

To qualify as a potential candidate for the NCE, you need a master's or higher degree with a major in counseling. The NBCC defines this as a degree where-in 48 semester hours (at minimum) in counseling cover at least nine requisite counseling coursework content domains. The degree has to include a course in professional orientation to counseling and a minimum of six semester hours of monitored field experience. You must have the equivalent of a counseling degree spanning 48 semesters or 72 hours of graduate-level credit, including a distinct counseling course in each of the following:

1. Human growth and development
2. Social and cultural foundations
3. Helping relationships
4. Group counseling processes and theories
5. Career counseling and lifestyle development
6. Counseling assessment
7. Research and program evaluation
8. Professional orientation to counseling

9. Field experience in counseling, wherein:
   a. Field experience must be the equivalent of a minimum of six semester hours or ten quarter hours of graduate credit.
10. Two years and a hundred hours of counseling supervision from someone with a master's or higher degree in the mental health discipline.

To ensure fairness, the NCE complies with the Americans with Disabilities Act and ensures that no one is deprived of taking the exam because of a disability. To that end, the examination partners provide accommodations for those with temporary or permanent disabilities or who do not have native/bilingual proficiency in English. To be eligible, you must submit a special accommodation request to your relevant state licensing board and get it reviewed and approved.

For special examination accommodations (SEA), you have to request this every time you register to take the exam. Pearson VUE is the official partner for administering and scoring the NCE. So, suppose you appear for the NCE with priorly approved special accommodation requests. In that case, you have to schedule the exam appointment via their toll-free number, 800-466-0450, and choose option three when prompted (National Counselor Examination (NCE) Handbook as Part of the National Certified Counselor (NCC) Application, 2023).

The NBCC has contracts with the Center for Credentialing and Education (CCE) concerning overseeing the examination procedure.

There are two options to register for the NCE (concerning state licensure). These are:

1. Online registration: To commence with this, you have to visit cce-global.org and click on the "Credentialing Gateway" option.
2. Paper registration: To request this form, you have to contact paperreg@cce-global.org. This specific method can take four additional processing weeks. A money order is the only payment method for paper registration.

If you do not test within the authorized window given to you once you register with CCE, you will be asked to surrender the registration and the fees you paid. Also, if you don't sit for the exam within your allotted window or your first attempt is unsuccessful, you can re-take it after a 90-day waiting period. After this, you can reregister at any time. You must pay the exam fee every time you reregister.

Online payments must be made by credit card (MasterCard, Visa, or American Express). If you go the paper registration route, you'll need a money order or cashier's check made payable to NBCC. The fees for the exam are non-refundable and non-transferable.

Let's go into the particulars involved in scheduling your exam.

Scheduling

After registering with the CCE, you will get authorization to test emails from Pearson VUE. This will also contain your candidate ID number. Following this, you can schedule an exam appointment online or by phone. A disclaimer— there may be a long hold time if you take the phone route. If you schedule online, follow these steps:

- Retrieve your candidate ID number from the email.
- Visit home.pearsonvnue.com/cce and choose the "Create Account" option.
- Follow the instructions to select your exam program and register.

If you schedule by phone, here are the steps you need to follow:

- Call 886-904-4432 (Pearson VUE) to schedule the exam appointment.
- This is toll-free, and you can call anytime between 7 a.m. and 7 p.m. Central Time on weekdays.

When you schedule an examination appointment, confirm a location for in-person testing. Tell them your preferred time and testing date, and give your client ID number. You'll be given some particulars, including the time you need to report to the test center or to report for testing. After you schedule the exam, you'll get a confirmation of registration mail from Pearson VUE. This will have your registration ID, date, appointment length, time, test center location, and any special accommodation requests that have been approved.

If you need to reschedule, you can call Pearson VUE. Once prompted, choose option three if you have any approved special accommodations. There is a $50 for rescheduling an exam.

Remember these particulars so you get the most bang for your buck:

- You will have to forfeit all registration and fees if you miss an appointment or do not reschedule at least 24 hours before the date you originally scheduled to take the exam.
- You must also forfeit fees and registration if you're over 15 minutes late to the exam.
- You cannot violate any Pearson VUE or NBCC/CCE rules or disobey a proctor or exam administrator.
- You must avoid any unethical or cheating behaviors during the registration and administration process.

If a personal emergency happens on the day of the exam, call CCE at 336-482-2856. A decision about qualifying for a retest will be made after a thorough review. If there is inclement weather, Pearson VUE will decide if the circumstances are enough to lead to canceling or rescheduling your exam appointment.

If it goes to the point where the test center people cannot open the facility, the exam will likely be rescheduled. If there are power cuts during the exam administration, it will restart at the last question that you completed. And if there are any interruptions or cancellations by a test center— although this is unusual— you will be notified by mail or telephone about rescheduling and reregistration.

Now let us go into the particulars of taking the exam.

Taking the Exam

There are specifics relevant to the chosen exam administration, whether you take the NCE in person or online. But before we get to those, let's take a minute to go over the general rules that apply to both these cases.

First of all, test takers who do any of the following can be dismissed from the exam on the grounds of **misconduct**:

- Disturbing others, being abusive, or showing a lack of cooperation during the exam
- Displaying or using electronic items such as cell phones, smart watches, personal digital assistants (PDAs), and pagers
- Helping or taking help from other test-takers
- Trying to record exam questions or take notes
- Trying to take the exam for someone else
- Getting caught with books, notes, or any other aids
- Partaking in data dump activities or misusing writing materials that are provided
- Engaging in any other behavior that the Pearson VUE exam administrator deems as a show of misconduct

If an examinee is found guilty of misconduct, they have to forfeit the exam scores and fees. Federal copyright law strictly prevents copying, reproducing, recording, distributing, displaying, or sharing any exam questions by any means whatsoever. All questions belong to the NBCC by copyright. People guilty of misusing questions incur misconduct penalties and can be tried for civil and criminal violations.

Before accessing any exam questions, candidates must read and consent to a nondisclosure agreement.

Coming to the **in-person exam administration**— This is delivered by computer at the selected Pearson VUE test center. You do not need any advanced computer experience or typing abilities to do this test. What you do need is to select answer choices. On the exam day, arrive at the center early so you have time to get your bearings in order. Before entering the test center, you must read and sign the Pearson VUE Candidate Agreement document, which details what you need to do if you require help with the exam policies or any other issues. Remember, if you are over 15 minutes late, you won't be allowed to take the exam and will have to forfeit the registration fee.

Pearson VUE test centers are selected on the basis of easy availability to all candidates. They are usually in all states and metropolitan areas. You can find the addresses and directions of the current centers at home.pearsonvue.com. Specific information pertaining to the location of your center will also be given to you once you register.

You need two identification forms. The first is a photo ID to get you admitted to the test center. The second is a valid government-issued ID. Remember the photo ID because without it, the admin will consider you a "missed appointment" case, and you won't get a refund of your exam fee. There is a high degree of security during the administration. The test center will be monitored by video and audio surveillance to ensure the following:

- No notes are being exchanged, and there's no use of cameras, tape recorders, personal digital assistants, cell phones, smartwatches, and pagers
- No calculators are being used
- No guests are coming to the testing room or reception areas (including family members)
- No personal effects, including valuables, are getting into the test center
- Proper administration of locker facilities for storing cell phones, wallets, and keys

Pearson VUE will not be responsible for items you leave in the reception areas, so be careful with how much you carry. Also, remember that they can decide if anything you're carrying is prohibited, so go as light as possible and only keep the essentials with you.

Writing materials will be handed to you once you check in. All these materials must be returned to the proctor once you complete your test. Without this, you won't get a score report. You cannot remove any notes or documents from the testing room. You also cannot ask any questions regarding the exam content. You can take breaks, but the clock will go on as it does— so any personal break could lead to a loss of time. Be vigilant with how much break time you need. Also, eating, chewing gum or tobacco, smoking, drinking, and vaping are all prohibited in the test center.

Once your ID is confirmed, you'll be taken to a testing cubicle. There will be video monitoring throughout the exam session. You'll see a nondisclosure agreement appear on the screen. You have to agree with the agreement terms to proceed with the exam, and you'll get five minutes to do this. Once you agree, there'll be a tutorial for the exam. Use the ten minutes you get to review how to navigate and answer the items well. Once you are ready, begin the exam by pressing "start."

You get three hours and 45 minutes to complete the exam. The computer will track what time you spend, and if you exceed the time limit, the exam will terminate. A digital clock will show you how much time you have left.

Only one exam question appears on the screen at a time. The question number will be in the upper right corner of the screen, and answer options are A, B, C, or D. Choose your answer by clicking the relevant alphabet with your mouse. If you change your mind, simply click on the other alphabet you deem the better choice. You can change answers as many times as you want within the exam time limit, but of course, the more programmed you become, the better. If you need to, you can go back to review questions. The NCE doesn't penalize guesswork, so try to provide an answer for each question.

If you take the exam **online (OnVUE)**, the initial procedures are the same. You don't need advanced typing or computer skills. You'll need to select answer choices. On the exam date, you can check in up to 30 minutes before the exam and 15 minutes after the appointment. Any later and you won't be allowed to take the exam or get a refund on fees. Before the exam begins, you have to read and sign the candidate agreement.

For identification, you'll get prompts to capture:

- A photo of your current valid government-issued ID, and
- A real-time picture of yourself

The first and last name you used to register for the exam **must** *match the first and last name on the government-issued ID you present on the exam day.* You can be asked to give an alternative if your ID does not pass the initial review. All IDs must be issued by the country where you take the test. Alternatively, you can use a passport from your country of citizenship with a secondary ID.

Without proper identification, your case will become a missed appointment, and you won't get a refund of the exam fee. So, before you schedule your exam, always make sure you have whatever documents you need.

Regarding security, you will need to take four photos of your testing environment. A VUE-certified proctor and artificial intelligence will do constant online monitoring or proctoring through webcam and microphone facilities. You must review the information you submit and follow up with a Pearson VUE team member if needed.

No one else (this includes children and animals except service animals) is allowed within the testing environment. Use a room that has a lock to reduce the possibility of interruptions. Any interruptions will lead to disqualification, in which case you'll have to schedule to take the exam at a test center on another date.

You will not be allowed to keep any cell phones, books, smart watches, or other materials that can compromise the test within the testing environment. This also includes white and bulletin boards and other items that could be considered a breach of procedure.

The Pearson VUE employee can give you other directives about the exam environment. Follow them to the T to avoid terminating the exam and forfeiting the appointment plus your fee.

You cannot ask any questions about the exam content during the examination. For onVUE exams, you cannot get up or leave the test computer barring one 15-minute prescheduled break. You will be offered a 15-minute break after the first 100 questions, but that is all. On returning from the break, you *will not* be allowed to return to any of the previous 100 questions. Once again, you cannot eat, chew gum, or smoke during the exam. You can keep water in a clear container on the testing surface.

Before the exam begins, review the test administration policies and rules from home.pearsonvue.com/cce/onvue. The proctor will need to see a full video of your testing location once your ID is confirmed.

As with the in-person test procedures, you will get a nondisclosure agreement that you need to sign within five minutes. This will be followed by an exam tutorial. After you've gone through these two formalities, begin your exam by clicking "start." You will get three hours and 45 minutes to finish the exam. Your computer will track the time you spend on the exam, and remember, it will terminate if you exceed the time limit.

A digital clock will indicate how much time you have left to complete your exam. Only one exam question will be given at a time. You will see the question number on the upper right side of the screen. You will get answer choices labeled A, B, C, or D. Indicate your choice by clicking any of them with your mouse. To change your answer, simply click the option that feels more relevant. Try to answer all questions because the NCE does not penalize guesswork.

Following The Exam

Once the exam is over, you will be asked to evaluate your experience briefly. After that, you will be instructed to report to the proctor to get your unofficial score report. This will include your photograph. Within a month after the end of the administration window, the CCE will report official scores to your licensing organization once they have verified your adherence to testing policies and procedures.

Scores will be reported in written form, not over the phone, by email, or by fax. You can order the report online in the Credentialing Gateway. NBCC, Pearson VUE, and CCE reserve the right to withdraw or declare official scores as null if there are any misconduct or rule violation reports.

Your performance on the NCE determines your exam score and is not dependent on or influenced by your work history, quality, or personal and professional variables. The methodology for determining the passing point is a modified Angoff method. Subject matter experts from the NCE Subject Matter Expert Committee make the responses and review numerical data to decide the appropriate pass mark. They evaluate every question to understand how many correct answers are needed to show a candidate has the KSA (knowledge, skills, and abilities) needed to pass.

The passing score and the marks you receive will be generated as a score report. The passing scores can vary slightly for every version of the exam. Once you get your scores, contact your state board for the next steps in licensure. Information about your test and results is confidential. If you want to appeal against your score, follow the appeals process set by the NBCC. This entails submitting a written request to the NBCC within 60 days of getting the exam results.

The request must have a detailed explanation of the basis for your appeal, plus any documentation that supports your case. Once the NBCC gets your request, they will review the appeal and decide if you can retake the exam. If you qualify for reevaluation, the exam will be rescored by an independent panel, and this time, the rescore results will be final.

With this, we come to the end of chapter one. In this chapter, we covered all the essentials you need to know when it comes to taking the NCE. The particulars are important if you are a first-timer because knowing the procedures before-hand will help you go into the exam preparation. On the day itself, you don't want to feel harassed and stressed because you missed something like your photo ID or accidentally brought your cell phone into the administering room. Take time to review this chapter because the basics are often the most important to ensure you keep a calm mind. In the next chapter, we will go into detail about preparing for the NCE.

Chapter Two: Preparing for the Exam

Preparing for anything challenging can be overwhelming. You know you are gearing up for something that could change your life and give you new openings, and this can feel scary. But with the right mindset and approach, readying yourself to take the NCE can be a stimulating opportunity to learn more about your knowledge and skills and hone them to become even better. As they say, pressure makes the diamond what it is.

Study Guide

The first step to acing the NCE is **preparing your course outline**. Begin by dividing the entire course's content into a definite number of sections or chapters. You can choose the divisions in this book, or you can make further divisions and subdivisions tailored to your needs. For instance, you can split a large chapter into two or three smaller subsections. This will make it easier to study. For the shorter chapters, you can do two or three of them at a time by merging them into a bigger section. Once you do this, you'll be able to allocate a good amount of time to each section without getting overwhelmed.

Make a note of the main topics in each module. Another great move is to analyze sample question papers from previous years. Do this to get an idea of which topics are most featured and which are least important.

The next step is to work on finding a priority basis. This means you have to narrow down the chapters and concepts that feel more important than others. Be subjective and objective about this.

Ensure you focus on critical and fundamental concepts. The best strategy to do well on tests without spending an excessive amount of time on questions is to memorize relevant information. One downside, however, is that many learners have a habit of forgetting information before an exam. You should single out topics that call for memorization and develop a unique strategy for them. Keep some time aside for periodic modifications depending on circumstantial changes as well.

Once this step is over, focus on **making a timetable**. Make a realistic timetable that will allow you to give ample time to each topic. Don't become too ambitious because you will get stressed trying to follow an overly complicated schedule. And make sure you break your studying hours into small intervals interspaced with breaks. To know how much time you have to devote to each chapter, consider these factors:

1. How many days are left for the exam? Mark this as A.
2. How many days/ hours do you have to miss studying for any other commitments? Mark this as B.
3. How many hours can you study every day? Mark this C.
4. From here, you will get a clear idea of how many hours you *actually* have to prepare for the exam. This will be (A-B)*C. Mark this as D.
5. Next, how many subjects are there? This is E.
6. Finally, get the total number of hours you can give to each subject by dividing D by E. Mark this as F.

Remember, this is only a rough assessment. You'll still need to rework bits and parts of the timeline depending on revisions and levels of difficulty. Plus, you'll also need some time to go over practice tests. This exercise is just to give you a basic idea of what you need to get familiarized with the exam's fundamentals. When you make your timetable, always leave a little wiggle room.

Once you've made a timetable, you have to focus on **self-assessment**. This will help you prepare to solve questions within an exam environment where time is limited and tensions run high. Begin by assessing your knowledge of each chapter by answering the questions feature at the end of it. If some are incorrect or you don't know their answers, go over the relevant topics again. Once you feel confident *and* answer everything correctly, move on to the next chapter.

After finishing the entire course, take some mock tests. You will find plenty of such tests online, and my book will also have two assessments styled off the NCE pattern to help you prepare better. When you sit for these tests, make sure your environment mimics the NCE environment. Remove any additional books and notes. Just keep the question paper (take a print of it if you need to) and answer sheets while you work.

For every assessment, there has to be a strategy. When you strategize, focus on finding approaches that'll help you get the maximum score. Consider these suggestions:

1. How will you start the paper?
2. What questions will you attempt at the beginning? Will you go in the order of the exam, the topics you know best, or the ones with the most marks?
3. What order will you follow in answering the paper?
4. What time will you give each part of the exam?
5. How much time do you need to leave for the last moment so you can relook and revise?

When you do the mock tests, begin by skimming through the entire paper. Divide time among the sections. Stick to the strategy you've planned for each section. Once you finish, analyze your work and check the questions you got wrong. Try to recall your mindset when you realize you may not get a particular question right. Consider what you could do differently to get more marks the next time.

And remember, it is always good to ask for help.

After you're done with the studying and mock tests, it's time to **study your performance and consider what you can do to get the most out of the exam**. Work on soft skills, including methods to improve self-confidence. Also, equip yourself to think and behave calmly during the exam with minimal anxiety. Your mental health should be at a place where it empowers you to take the exam efficiently and with concentration.

Begin by comprehensively analyzing the assessments you take. The NCE tests more than your knowledge. It also studies your attitudes and overall ability to perform under pressure. The approach you take is most important. Consider some things right at the onset:

- What should you do the second the exam begins? I always feel it is best to take two seconds and a *deep, deep breath*. Tell yourself you got this.
- What will you do in the last 15 minutes of the exam? Should you keep some time aside to review what you've answered? Or are you confident enough to leave it as it is? Remember, this is subjective, although I'd say a quick revision can help you spot any errors you may have made the first time around.

One of the biggest challenges of the NCE is learning to handle exam pressure. It is hard when your career is hinged on this, I get it. But look at it this way—stress won't make it any easier. Practice handling and navigating through the pressure by doing as many mock tests as you can. Model the exam environment each time. I find that it helps to work on little exercises that can improve your concentration.

Finally, train your mind to think positively. If there is something negative, take another deep breath and remind yourself it's just a thought and it has *no hold* on your capabilities. A positive, happy mind will learn quicker and be more confident when taking the exam.

What will you do **a week before the main exam**? The most important period to study for the NCE test is the last week before you take it. Take a methodical approach this week to getting your head in the game for the decisive showdown.

The first step in getting your brain to operate quicker on the test is to relax mindfully. Cut your study time by at least half. Get plenty of sleep and aim to be well-rested at all times. Both a peaceful state of mind and restful sleep are necessary. Time must be set aside for regular revisions so that they are kept in mind while writing the paper. YouTube can be of great help.

Don't try to learn anything new. It's best to recall the information you already know. Make the most of what you are already familiar with by reviewing it thoroughly at this time. Confusion over new material and a lack of confidence throughout the test are inevitable results of trying to cram in too much new information at the last moment.

Temper what you see and hear on social media. Many things you learn through your television, newspaper, and social media feeds are very unsettling and can ruin your peace of mind. To keep yourself free from unnecessary worries, always take a very cautious approach to sensational gossip, news, and shows at this time. You don't need to be bombarded with new and irrelevant information ahead of the NCE, so do this for yourself.

Take two or three practice tests in the week leading up to the NCE, and aim to finish each one in the allotted time. This will train your brain to focus on finishing your assignment at a certain time. It will also help you feel more confident going into the final test. A disclaimer: on the final day before the exam, minimize everything else. Prepare all you need-- including your ID card and what you must carry. Check the list of essentials and what you shouldn't have on your person. And get plenty of sleep.

Before the final, you should lay the groundwork for your final test strategy. Be flexible with your study strategies in case the test throws a wrench into your preparations. The main strategy should include deciding a) which sections to do first, b) which sections to do last, c) what to do with the hardest and easiest questions, and d) which types of questions to spend the most time on and which types to spend the least.

Now that you've reached the ultimate step, the question is, what do you do when you're giving the exam? You breathe, and you tell yourself you have everything it takes to do amazingly and get a great score. Your primary objective right now is to stay calm and have faith in your abilities.

Studying for the NCE

Studying for the NCE is meant to test you. It's completely natural to be worried. Some of the best things you can do during the preparation phase are to take time to understand the test format and content, consider test prep options, and build good studying habits.

The test format will help you get a clear idea of how the exam will look on the final day. The NCE has 200 multiple-choice questions. You get three hours and 45 minutes to finish all of them. Forty out of the total 200 are field-tested, and these will not be scored. The maximum possible score is 160. These questions will test your overall adaptiveness to becoming an effective counselor. This means you need to understand what it entails as a job, have empathy for any and all clients, and be objective and informed in your decision-making.

You have to be aware of what will be going into the test. I have highlighted each of these areas in the previous chapter, but let's quickly brush up. The 200 questions will be derived from 13 subjects. Each of these is determined by the CACREP and are essential knowledge area.

The subjects are further based on eight content areas and six work behaviors. You will have access to many resources when it comes to studying the 13 subjects. Of course, this book will equip you with all the essentials. For additional studying, you can refer to the NBCC's official preparation guide. Study packages from the *Association for Advanced Training in the Behavioral Sciences* are also beneficial.

Finally, you should model an ideal studying behavior. You already have an idea about what will work and what won't. But just to help streamline everything, here are some basic studying tips:

- Find a calm and good studying environment with minimal distractions.
- Focus on being cool and collected when you study.
- Practice relaxation techniques so you know how to stay composed during the main exam.
- Talk to your friends and other professionals and those who have taken the exam or are studying for it. They can give you their insight and maybe offer helpful tips.
- Lastly, never forget self-care. It is so tempting to pull all-nighters, but in my experience, they cause burnout and can lead to nervous breakdowns before the main event. You don't want to exhaust your energy reserve, so always take breaks, sleep eight hours, and nourish yourself with good food. Watch good films that don't promote violence or overly excite you. And practice self-affirmations to increase your confidence.

We have reached the end of chapter two. In this chapter, you learned about the essential things you need to do to be prepared on the day of the exam. Very often, I have found that many of us do well right until the night before an exam. We study, we take important notes, and we do everything right.

Then, at the last moment, we begin to panic, thinking we're not good enough. This means we sabotage ourselves. This comes through as a blackout on the main day. We look at the questions, and we *know* we've studied them, but somehow, it feels like drawing a blank. As counselors, I believe that we are intrinsically empathic people. This means we feel and experience emotions intensely.

It is essential not to let this overwhelm us and to treat the exam as a means to become the best professional version of ourselves. My best advice is to go hard until the very last day before the NCE. That day, just prepare your bag and make sure you have all your essential items. Once you've done that, take a step back and relax. There is nothing more you can learn or change because you *are* ready.

In the next chapter, we will move into the first out of the eight common core areas of the NCE, which is Professional Orientation and Ethical Practice.

Chapter Three: Professional Orientation and Ethical Practice

Professionalism and ethics constitute the backbone of any practice, including counseling. This is the chapter where you learn to identify your moral compass. As a counselor, you must be able to maintain objective neutrality while you help your patients navigate through different situations to come out feeling like they can and deserve to live wholesome lives.

Counseling Defined

Counseling is an individualized, personalized form of assistance that involves personal, vocational, and educational elements. Counselors study pertinent facts and analyze and interpret them depending on the kind of case they are presented with.

Historical Overview

The development of counseling throughout time has been gradual and intricate. This background is crucial for the NCE test because it puts modern counseling practices and their underlying theoretical frameworks in perspective.

Ancient cultures like Egypt and Greece developed their own versions of counseling. Egyptians, for instance, believed in studying and interpreting dreams to understand how the mind worked, while the Greeks engaged in intellectual debates.

Sigmund Freud established psychoanalysis in the 19th century to unearth the patient's underlying motivations and feelings. Freud's thoughts and techniques have and continue to significantly influence the area of counseling.

Counseling ideas such as behaviorism, which emphasized using reward and punishment to alter behavior, and humanistic psychology, which hinged on the values of self-actualization and development, arose in the early to mid-1900s (Walinga, 2014).

The counseling profession exploded in the 1950s and '60s with the advent of innovative techniques, including solution-focused brief treatment (SFBT), cognitive-behavioral therapy (CBT), and family therapy (Macdonald, 2011). These methods emphasized the importance of the counselor-client partnership.

Counselors in the 1970s and 1980s rediscovered an interest in multiculturalism and diversity because they observed a growing need to help clients of various backgrounds overcome their own difficulties. Multicultural counseling emerged as a result, recognizing the significance of a client's background in their emotional well-being (Ford et al., 2015).

Counseling has evolved and adapted to new cultural and social norms in the modern day. Online counseling and smartphone applications are becoming more accessible as the value of using technology in therapy is more acknowledged. Treating mental health issues continues to be necessary, but there is also an increased focus on critical co-related areas like facilitating overall wellness and discovering means of prevention.

Here is a brief table of notable historical events that have influenced the discipline as we know it today:

- 1879: The first psychosocial laboratory was established by Wilhelm Wundt.
- 1890: Sigmund Freud began using psychoanalysis to treat mental illness.
- 1898: Jesse Davis started working as a professional counselor at Detroit High School.

- 1908: Clifford Beers wrote *A Mind That Found Itself,* which exposed conditions within mental health institutions.
- 1908: Frank Parsons directed the Vocation Bureau based in Boston.
- 1909: *Choosing A Vocation* was published by Frank Parsons, and this established the trait-factor approach to guidance, which matches individual abilities to career paths. This approach is based on the assumption that we all have certain capabilities that make us more suited to one occupation over the other, which is what this kind of counseling aims to help us discover.
- 1913: The National Vocational Guidance Association was founded as the first counseling association.
- 1917: Smith-Hughes Act granted federal funds for guidance and vocational education.
- 1927: The Strong-Vocational Interest Blank was published. The Strong Interest Inventory (SII) is a popular tool for career assessment relevant to the trait-factor guidance approach. It was developed by E. K. Strong and has gone through multiple revisions. It assesses individual interests in six core areas: investigative, realistic, social, enterprising, artistic, and conventional (The Myers-Briggs Company, 2019). These are then used to match a person with a potential career path that is in tune with their interests.
- 1939: Parsons' trait-factor approach was modified by E. G. Williamson in his publication *How To Counsel Students.*
- 1942: Publication of *Counseling And Psychotherapy* by Carl Rogers.
- 1945: Post World War II, counseling services to veterans in the Veterans Affairs (VA) agency were expanded.
- 1951: The American Personnel and Guidance Association came into existence.
- 1954: The Office of Vocational Rehabilitation was created.
- 1958: The National Defense Education Act was passed. This made financial resources available for school counselor training.
- The 1960s: New theoretical approaches came into existence, including rational emotive, gestalt, behavioral, and reality.
- 1962: *The Counselor in a Changing World* was published by Gilbert Wrenn. It emphasized counseling to be a profession focusing on developmental needs.
- 1976: The State of Virginia passed the first licensure law for general practice counselors.

- 1981: The Council for the Accreditation of Counseling and Related Educational Programs (CACREP) was established.
- The 1980s: Licensure and certification credentials for counseling increased.
- 1983: The American Group Psychotherapy Association became American Association for Counseling and Development (AACD). It would go on to become American Counseling Association (ACA) in 1992.
- The 1990s: Counseling would begin expanding services, leading to the rise of specialty areas.
- The 1990s: More federal legislation would recognize counseling to be a distinct profession.
- 2000s: There would be more than 55,000 certified counselors at the national level and over 110,000 licensed counselors.
- 2010: California passed legislation for counselor licensure. At present, all 50 states and the District of Columbia, and Puerto Rico, have licensure.
- 2011-2020: Ongoing concerns include licensure portability, professional identity development, and CACREP's role in setting standards.

CACREP Standards

In contemporary counseling, a continuing issue surrounds the values, roles, and influence exerted by the CACREP, which is the agency for national counselor accreditation. Since counseling as a profession is seeking more unity and recognition, both within and outside the profession, it looks at CACREP as a unifying force (CACREP, 2016). Outside constituencies, including licensure authorities, academic institutions, and hiring bodies, have begun including or needing CACREP program graduation as an admission and eligibility requirement. The issue is related to the several professional counselors who have not graduated from or are in a non-CAREP program. Some states are progressing to license only CACREP graduates as *professional* counselors.

Counselor education programs are more and more hinged on seeking accreditation from the CACREP. The accredited program's curriculum and objectives must be attuned to approved standards alongside clinical instruction. Faculty, as well as staff, have to meet CACREP standards covering administrative structures and organizations (CACREP, 2016). The college embracing this program must also be willing to partake in program evaluations determined by CACREP standards.

Graduates of CACREP-accredited courses are equipped for positions in mental health, human services, learning, private practice, the military, government business, and industry. Graduates of entry-level counseling programs are qualified to practice counseling and for applicable credentialing (e.g., licensing, certification). Graduates at the doctoral level are equipped for roles in counseling academia, supervision, investigation, and higher-level practice.

The 2024 CACREP Standards have been organized into six sections.

1. The Learning Environment covers standards related to institutional and program structure and resources.
2. Academic Quality gives a framework to help student assessment and program evaluation.
3. The Foundational Counseling Curriculum has a statement pertaining to unified professional counselor identities. In addition, it also has standards for the education program curriculum of entry-level counselors. This is what constitutes the eight core content areas influencing the content of the NCE.
4. Professional Practice encapsulates standards mandated for practice at the entry-level and the composition and delivery of field experiences.
5. Entry-Level Specialized Practice Areas generate standards regarding the necessary knowledge and skills for specialty areas. This includes specialized practice areas accredited by the CACREP, including career, addictions, clinical mental health, rehabilitation counseling, marriage, couple, and family, school counseling, and college counseling.
6. Doctoral Standards for Counselor Education and Supervision cover the learning environment, doctoral-level internship needs, and professional identity (pertaining to doctoral-level graduates).

The CACREP standards form a solid foundation for a professional counselor's education. They help you to build and maintain a professional identity while learning about cultural and social diversity, human growth and development, helping relationships, research, assessment, program evaluation, and group work. The **professional practice standards** will need you, as a counselor, to be well-versed with mental health care theory and its application (CACREP, 2016). At the graduate level, you have to be willing to accept entry-level positions to become adept at all skills. A standard criteria set helps assess whether a graduate student has maxim professional proficiency. This set includes:

- Meeting requirements of accreditation
- Follow ethical standards of practice to help and benefit the public
- Achieving all competencies mandated to practice at entry level
- Completing academic classes satisfactorily
- Completing a supervised clinical experience satisfactorily (this is usually 3,000 hours)
- Meeting all necessary provisions for certifications

Other Current And Continuing Trends

In contemporary counseling, numerous events, natural phenomena, and situations have increased interest in trauma, crisis, and disaster counseling. Situations like war, terrorism, natural disasters, and other events that lead to trauma need niche mental health diagnostic skills and interventions. In 2010, a national convention was held by the American Counseling Association (ACA), following which a new program category known as *Disaster Mental Health* got established (American Counseling Association, 2019). As of now, revisions of the CACREP incorporate counselor training standards relevant to disaster, crisis, and trauma counseling.

The definition and scope of practice of counseling continue to be dynamic. The discipline defines interest and competence areas such as spirituality, multiculturalism, violence and trauma, crises, wellness, and technology. The scope will always remain dynamic due to changing state laws and the influence of other professions on how counseling is delivered.

Social justice is an expanding concept. It addresses issues such as unearned privilege, inequality of power, and oppression and aims to promote a greater balance of power and resources. Advocacy competencies for counselors are identified by ACA and implemented within counselor training modules.

Today, counselors need an acute awareness of the relationship between the functions of our bodies, nourishment, medication and drugs, and concurrent mental behavior and states. Many ways we behave can be rooted in brain and biological functions that cannot be overlooked for diagnoses and counseling purposes. To ensure cognizance, the trend is manifested through coursework in training programs, seminars, and professional workshops.

Finally, distance counseling through different media tools is becoming more and more entrenched. Numerous social media tools can be used as supplementary ways to build, maintain, and enhance a counseling relationship. The ACA has published guidelines on this area in its Code of Ethics.

ACA Advocacy Competencies

The American Counseling Association (ACA) updates its advocacy competencies on a regular basis to reflect developments in the counseling profession as well as the larger social and political climate (Ratts et al., 2010). Here are some examples of key competencies:

- Advocating for policies promoting fairness, justice, and client and community well-being.
- Employing evidence-based methods to educate advocacy activities and support successful policies and programs.
- Building coalitions and alliances with various stakeholders to promote common aims.
- Protecting client confidentiality and autonomy by applying ethical concepts and standards to advocacy activities.
- Recognizing and resolving structural obstacles to access and equality in counseling service delivery.
- Advocating for constructive changes in laws, rules, and policies at the local, state, and national levels.
- Employing advocacy techniques and tactics such as grassroots organization, lobbying, and media outreach.
- Evaluating the effectiveness of lobbying activities on a regular basis and alter methods as required to obtain the desired results.
- Continuing long-term advocacy activities encourage counselor self-care and resilience.

- Using technology and social media to spread advocacy messages to a wider audience.

These skills highlight the significance of advocacy in the counseling profession, as well as the necessity for counselors to participate in advocacy initiatives that promote social justice, equality, and well-being for their clients and communities. The competencies are further subdivided into groups.

Client/ Student Empowerment

1. An advocacy acclimation includes system change interventions and empowerment strategy implementation in direct counseling.
2. Counselors oriented toward advocacy have to recognize social, political, cultural, and economic impacts on human development.
3. They also have to aid their students and clients understand their lives in this larger developmental context.
4. This forms the grounds of self-advocacy.

Empowerment Counselor Competencies

From the perspective of indirect interventions, a counselor can:

1. Identify resources and strengths of students and clients.
2. Identify different political, economic, social, and cultural factors impacting clients and students.
3. Recognize signs indicating individual behaviors and concerns reflect responses to oppression.
4. Help individuals identify external barriers at appropriate developmental levels that could impact their development.
5. Train clients and students to self-advocate.
6. Help them develop action plans for self-advocacy.
7. Assist clients and students in carrying out action plans

Client/Student Advocacy

1. Counselors may take on an advocacy role when they identify external factors that impede an individual's progress.
2. This can involve advocating for policies and programs that promote the client's well-being and help remove obstacles to their development.
3. In particular, counselors may act as advocates for clients or students who face difficulties accessing necessary services or resources, especially those who belong to vulnerable populations.

Client/Student Advocacy Counselor Competencies

In situations needing environmental interventions on behalf of students and clients, a counselor should be able to:

1. Negotiate relevant education systems and services on their behalf.
2. Help them access required resources.
3. Identify barriers to well-being.
4. Develop a primary plan of action to tackle the barriers.
5. Identify potential allies for confronting barriers.
6. Carry out the primary action plan.

Community Collaboration

1. The ongoing work of counselors with people makes them aware of recurring themes.
2. Counselors are frequently among the first people to gain awareness of environmental difficulties.
3. Advocacy-oriented counselors can respond to challenges by alerting organizations working for change that are also interested in the existing issues.
4. The counselor's primary role here is as an ally.
5. Counselors can also make particular skills available to organizations, including communications, interpersonal relations, training, and research.

Community Collaboration Counselor Competencies

1. Identifying environmental components harming the development of clients and students.
2. Alerting community and school groups with common concerns related to the existing issue.
3. Developing alliances with groups advocating change.
4. Using effective listening skills to comprehend group goals.
5. Identifying resources and strengths that group members bring to systemic change.
6. Communicating recognition and acknowledgment of these resources and strengths.
7. Locating and offering skills that can help groups.
8. Assessing the impact of their interactions within the community.

Systems Advocacy

1. When counselors locate systemic factors that are barriers to development, they may want to change the environment and prevent some of these problems from re-occurring.
2. Regardless of the specific target, processes for altering the status quo bear common qualities. Change needs persistence, communication and collaboration, vision, leadership, strong data, and systems analysis. In many situations, the counselor is the right person to offer leadership.

Systems Advocacy Counselor Competencies

An advocacy-oriented counselor can identify environmental factors while exerting systems-change leadership at school or community levels. This includes:

1. Identifying environmental components hurting the development of students and clients.
2. Providing and interpreting data demonstrating the urgency for change.
3. Collaborating with other stakeholders to develop a vision for guiding change.
4. Analyzing the sources of political and social influence and power within a system.

5. Developing a detailed plan for implementing this change.
6. Developing a plan for dealing with likely responses to change.
7. Recognizing and handling resistance.
8. Assessing the impact of their advocacy efforts on the overall system and its constituents.

Information to the Public

1. Professional counselors exchange knowledge of human development and communication competence across contexts, specializations, and theoretical viewpoints.
2. These characteristics enable advocacy-oriented counselors to raise public awareness of systemic challenges concerning human dignity.

Competencies of a Public Information Counselor

The advocacy-oriented counselor is able to:

1. Recognize the influence of oppression and other impediments to healthy development by enlightening the public about the importance of environmental variables in human development.
2. Determine environmental elements that promote healthy growth.
3. Prepare written and multimedia materials that explain the role of specific environmental factors in human development in detail.
4. Communicate information ethically and suitably for the intended demographic.
5. Disseminate information through various mediums.
6. Identify and cooperate with other experts active in public information dissemination.
7. Examine the impact of the counselor's public communication activities.

Social/Political Advocacy

1. Counselors often serve as catalysts for change in the systems that directly influence their students and clients.
2. This experience frequently leads to the realization that a few of the issues they have addressed have impacted individuals in a much bigger context.

3. Counselors utilize their expertise in carrying out social/political activism when this occurs.

Competencies of a Social/Political Advocacy Counselor

The advocacy-oriented counselor is able to distinguish those issues that can best be handled by social/political action when influencing public policy in a big public arena. This involves their ability to:

1. Determine the best processes and approaches for dealing with these issues.
2. Find and join forces with possible allies.
3. Support existing change alliances.
4. Set up persuasive data and change rationales with allies; lobby legislators and other policymakers with allies.
5. Maintain an open line of communication with communities and customers to ensure that social/political activism is in line with the original aims.

Profession

A counselor is someone with professional training in counseling, social work, psychology, or nursing. They specialize in one or multiple counseling areas. This can be rehabilitation, vocation, education, substance abuse, relationship, marriage, or family counseling (among others). As a counselor, your role is to provide professional advice, evaluation, and suggestions that will enhance your clients' ability to solve issues, make informed decisions, and bring about desired changes in their behavior and attitudes. Today, attitudes and perceptions of different professions toward counseling have changed. In human resources, for instance, counselors are recognized as professionals who can help employees by offering short-term counsel on work and performance-related issues. Let us look at the different kinds of counselors.

First, we have **professional counselors**. Their nature is dependent on the following components:

1. A defined objective list regarding their position with instructions on how to meet the said objectives.

2. Relevant training techniques will be applied to meet individual requirements. These techniques are founded on the principles of law, theology, and science and cannot be applied by laypeople.
3. Membership in a professional institution or organization.
4. Service-oriented ethical operation geared to help others perform better.

Then, there are **mental health counselors**. In the early 1980s, they received little recognition due to the Office of Civilian Health and Medical Program policies for the Uniformed Services, now TRICARE. Opponents found that the lack of a uniform certification and licensure system was troublesome. Today, managed care programs have greatly streamlined processes, enabling states to respond by passing licensure legislation. Both the professional and mental health counselor titles became more popular in the 1990s. The mental health counselors' responsibilities were defined in the 1981 manual of the American Mental Health Counselors Association (AMHCA). The job description of the mental health counselor was noted in the Occupational Outlook Handbook and the Dictionary of Occupational Titles in 1984.

Counselor educators serve as a bridge of understanding between mental health researchers and practitioners. Educators help their students understand research rationale and also help a researcher to understand the importance of ethical and sound counseling practices. They may do this by providing a student with assignments delving into cognitive therapy procedures.

Psychiatrists are qualified medical doctors who have four years of residence in the field of psychiatry. They assess and prescribe treatment options for complex mental illnesses. They also provide consultation for other mental health service providers and can often work alongside a counselor, who takes care of the therapy aspect of treatment. Psychiatrists can conduct psychoanalysis and psychotherapy to hospitalize clients, prescribe medications, and order tests.

Aside from psychiatrists, **psychiatric nurses** are the only healthcare providers with medical experience, mental health instruction, and training. The psychiatric nurse works closely with those who are experiencing severe emotional disorders. The psychiatrist keeps the psychiatric nurse accountable for delivering excellent medical treatment and drug administration.

Clinical psychologists are mental health specialists who specialize in evaluating, diagnosing, and treating psychological problems and mental disease. They assist people, couples, households, and organizations in improving their mental health and well-being. Clinical psychologists often use many evidence-based therapies, including cognitive-behavioral, psychodynamic, and interpersonal therapy. They are not permitted to prescribe drugs in most states in the United States.

A few states, however, have approved laws allowing highly qualified psychologists to prescribe drugs in specific circumstances. Clinical psychologists may prescribe drugs in Louisiana, New Mexico, Idaho, Colorado, Iowa, and Illinois, and the U.S. territory of Guam. In these regions, they must finish further training and fulfill other particular standards to prescribe drugs. The state psychological board and the state medical board also govern them. A larger percentage of clinical psychologists collaborate with psychiatrists or equivalent licensed medical practitioners who can prescribe drugs.

Finally, we have **social workers**. Social workers are professionals who assist individuals, families, and communities in tackling a variety of social and emotional concerns. They take a comprehensive approach to helping clients enhance their quality of life by offering therapy, representation, and connections to community resources. Social workers may work in various contexts, including healthcare facilities, educational institutions, government organizations, and non-profit groups. Social workers are bound by an ethical code that stresses the significance of social justice, diversity, and the advancement of human rights.

The CACREP

The Council for Accreditation of Counseling and Related Educational Programs (CACREP) was founded in 1981. It is in charge of certifying master's and doctoral-level counseling training programs to assure professional competence and the preparation of future practitioners. CACREP promotes the continuous assessment and advancement of academic and professional practice programs. The majority of state licensing bodies broadly approve the CACREP criteria. The Council on Rehabilitation Education (CORE), an official affiliate of CACREP, has embraced Clinical Rehabilitation Counseling criteria.

Specific CORE programs may also be eligible for clinical mental health program certification. CACREP standards were revised and released in 2016. The current requirements identify six master's level programs: addictions, career, clinical mental health, marriage, couple and family, school and student affairs, and college. Counselor education and supervision is the only Ph.D. program recognized by CACREP. There are roughly 700 recognized programs in the United States, with many schools having two or more and approximately 60 accredited doctorate programs.

Certification

As a voluntary process of title control, certification recognizes an individual with specific predetermined qualifications. For instance, the designation "National Certified Counselor (NCC)" controls the "Certified" word. Others cannot use this without the threat of an impending lawsuit by the one who does the certification.

The NBCC

The National Board for Certified Counselors, Inc. (NBCC) provides generic counselor certification. Requirements for this include a master's in counseling, coursework in eight areas of content, pre-degree experiences in the field, and 3,000 hours of post-degree work experience (supervised) over a two-year period (*How Long Does It Take to Become a Licensed Counselor?*, n.d.). In addition, the candidate must successfully pass the NCE. Specialty counselor certification can also be had in the following areas (after successful completion of an exam):

1. National Certified School Counselor (NCSC)

2. Certified Clinician Mental Health Counselor (CCMHC)

3. Master Addictions Counselor (MAC)

The NBCC mandates continuing education units to be certified. There are 100 clock hours for every five certification years.

Graduates in counseling who are nearing the end of their programs can apply for the NCE. If they come from a CACREP program, they can be certified on graduation without post-degree experience in work. Those in non-CACREP programs become board eligible upon graduating and have to gather 3,000 hours of post-degree work experience.

Other certifying bodies include the Commission on Rehabilitation Counselor Certification and States that certify school counselors, alcohol and drug counselors, and other counseling-specific groups.

Licensure

Licensure pertains to the passage of state legislation that governs a profession's practice and/or title (for example, counseling). During this process, a state grants an individual permission to practice counseling (as defined by state law) and use a title such as Licensed Professional Counselor. At the national level, there is no licensing system in place. A master's degree in counseling, courses in the eight core areas, pre-degree field experiences, post-degree supervised counseling job experience, and successful completion of a test are the general prerequisites for nationwide licensing.

The criteria differ from one state to the next. For licensing, most states utilize the National Counselor Examination, some others use the National Clinical Mental Health Counseling Examination, and a few accept either test. Most states possess title and practice control rules, ensuring no one may practice counseling without a license.

Several states have "title-control" laws, meaning anyone can practice counseling but cannot legally use the title (e.g., Licensed Professional Counselor) unless licensed. State regulations govern licensing. You may be licensed in many states at the same time. For licensing renewal, most states demand continuing education hours. Counselors are licensed in all 50 states, the District of Columbia, and Puerto Rico.

Some risks to counselor licenses include the narrowing of practice areas for counselors as state licensure regulations are amended and proposed revisions to several states' legislation.

In credentialing, there is a process called **reciprocity**. This is when one credentialing agency accepts the credential of another agency equivalent to it. For instance, a state licensure board can accept another state's license to be equivalent. Some states also refer to this as an **endorsement** (Patel & Sharma, 2019).

Confidentiality and Privileged Communication

Confidentiality, an ethical concept, is the privacy extended in a counseling relationship by the counselor to their patient. It must be respected. Privileged communication, a legal concept, is given to counselors when passing a state law like a licensure law. It is a legal right to privileged communication between a counselor and a client. It is similar to the kind of privilege exercised in psychology, medical, and legal occupations (Nguyen, 2019). It means that if the counselor has to testify in a court of law, they do not have to reveal the nature and content of their interactions with their client during counseling. Privileged communication may be broken under some circumstances, including if:

1. The client poses a threat to themselves or others.
2. There is child neglect or abuse.
3. The client requests for counseling records to be released.
4. A lawsuit is filed against the counselor.
5. The material is employed in the supervision.
6. Involuntary hospitalization is in the cards.
7. The release of information has been mandated by a court.

Duty to Warn

After Tatiana Tarasoff was killed by Prosenjit Poddar, the client of a university psychologist, the Tarasoff family filed a lawsuit against the University of California Board of Regents. Poddar had vowed to murder Tarasoff throughout the discussion. In this 1976 case, a California court decided that failing to warn a potential victim was professionally irresponsible (Cherry, 2019). In such cases, you must violate confidentially (and relinquish privileges if you have any) and notify the intended victim(s). Clearly, the counselor's ability to accurately and effectively discern the client's objectives is crucial. Other states' courts have typically confirmed and built on this historic legal ruling.

Duty to Protect

In the event of suicidal clients, the client must be protected. Formal operational procedures and referral alternatives should be established ahead of time (Granich, 2014). The following are some indicators to consider when determining the gravity of suicide risk:

- Direct verbal warnings and previous attempts
- A specific plan in place and the means at hand (gun, pills, etc.)
- Despair and a feeling of helplessness
- Donating possessions
- A history of drug or alcohol misuse

The obligation to protect extends to other individuals, such as children, the elderly, and those with physical or mental impairments in most states.

Other Important Terms

In ten US states and the District of Columbia, **physician-assisted suicide** is allowed. It is a legal choice in Oregon, Colorado, New Jersey, the District of Columbia, Hawaii, New Mexico, Maine, Vermont, and Washington. It is a legal option available to people in Montana and California. Individuals must have a terminal condition and a life expectancy of six months or fewer. Physicians cannot be penalized for giving drugs that accelerate death (CNN Library, 2020).

A statement of disclosure and informed consent in counseling is a document that informs clients about the therapy process, the counselor and client's roles and duties, and the potential dangers and benefits of counseling. It also describes the client's privacy and confidentiality rights and their limitations.

The disclosure and informed consent statement are meant to ensure that clients have all the details about the counseling procedure and may make an educated decision regarding participation. Clients are requested to sign the paper to indicate that they have read and comprehended the material presented and agree to engage in therapy. The disclosure statement could also contain facts about the counselor's qualifications, price structure, termination policy, and any additional pertinent rules or processes. It is an essential aspect of the therapy process because it builds confidence and clarity.

Counselors can be held **legally responsible and sued** for causing harm to their clients through various means, including causing mental distress, engaging in sexual harassment or misconduct, being negligent, making false claims about their professional services, or committing battery. Malpractice occurs when a counselor fails to provide professional services or provides services that fall below the standard expected of a professional in similar circumstances. For a malpractice claim to be successful in court, the following four conditions must be met:

1. A professional relationship must have been established.
2. There must have been a breach of duty on the part of the counselor.
3. The client must have suffered physical or psychological harm.
4. The harm must have been caused by the counselor's breach of duty.

The **Family Educational Rights and Privacy Act (1974)** is also known as the Buckley Amendment. Its purpose is to protect individual privacy. It makes provisions for parents under the age of 18 and students, if they are a minimum of 18 years old, to have access to data in their education records. This does not include counseling records.

Title IX of the educational amendments is a 1972 legislation banning sex discrimination in schools, academics, and athletics. The primary goal of this regulation has been to provide women with equal chances in sports as males. Women must have equal participation chances.

Managed health care refers to requirements promoted by insurance companies for reducing health care costs. This covers strict adherence to policies like record-keeping, treatment plans, and diagnosis. Mental health workers, including social workers, counselors, and psychologists, apply for a provider list status that is managed by Preferred Provider Organizations (PPOs) and Health

Maintenance Organizations (HMOs). Without doing this, they many lose out on potential clients.

The **Affordable Care Act** was created to enhance health insurance affordability and quality. It also aimed to expand public and private insurance coverage to lower the uninsured rate, as well as reduce healthcare costs for individuals and the government. Various measures such as mandates, subsidies, and insurance exchanges were established to achieve these goals and improve coverage and affordability. Under the new standards, insurance companies are required to cover all applicants and offer equal rates.

The act also mandates that mental health care services be treated similarly to regular health care services, extending the Mental Health Parity and Addiction Equity Act of 2008.

The **Health Insurance Portability and Accountability Act (HIPPA)** is a national law for protecting patient information in healthcare. This includes psychotherapy records covering medication, diagnosis and clinical tests, and treatment information. Clients need to sign a document indicating they have been told about the HIPPA rules.

The Paul Wellstone and Pete Domenici Mental Health Parity and Addiction Equity Act is a federal law covering:

* Private sector health plans that cover 50 or more employees
* State and local government plans that are not self-insured

It states these bodies have to provide the same coverage levels to individuals with addiction and mental health issues as those with surgical and medical issues.

TRICARE enables active as well as retired members of military service and their families to acquire services from a TRICARE-certified counselor without needing a physician to give them a referral or seeing them first.

The **Veteran's Administration** approves hiring licensed professional counselors. They can practice independently in different VA institutions if they are experienced (one or more years of mental health counseling).

Code of Ethics

A profession's statement of what it considers right and wrong in terms of professional behavior is labeled as the relevant code of ethics for it. Many of the ACA Code of Ethics' rules of conduct are frequently included in state statutes governing counselor licensing. Indeed, several states now require licensed counselors to adhere to the ACA Code of Ethics.

Counselors are required to adhere to a set of ethical standards to ensure they provide effective and professional services while maintaining confidentiality and protecting their client's rights. These ethical standards include:

1. Confidentiality: Counselors must keep all information about their clients confidential, except in cases where the law requires them to disclose information.
2. Informed Consent: Counselors must obtain informed consent from clients before providing any services and provide them with all relevant information about the services.
3. Boundaries: Counselors must establish clear boundaries with their clients to ensure the therapeutic relationship remains professional and does not cross any personal or social boundaries.
4. Competence: Counselors must maintain their knowledge and skills to provide competent services to their clients.
5. Multicultural Competence: Counselors must be aware of and respect their client's cultural backgrounds and provide culturally appropriate services.
6. Dual Relationships: Counselors must avoid dual relationships with their clients that could potentially cause harm or create a conflict of interest.
7. Records: Counselors must maintain accurate and secure records of their clients and ensure their confidentiality.
8. Professional Responsibility: Counselors must take responsibility for their professional actions and be accountable for their behavior.

These ethical standards are established by professional organizations, including the American Counseling Association (ACA).

Questions and Answers

Finish all the questions in this section to test your competence before moving to the next chapter.

1. A woman requests your help with an eating disorder, but you are not experienced in this area. Ethically, you should:

    A. Refer her to a colleague who is trained and experienced in this area
    B. Keep the client and try to improve their self-esteem
    C. Tell the client you will do a comprehensive study on the topic and then see her
    D. Explain that eating or not eating is not the real problem and that counseling will help uncover real underlying issues

2. Regarding state law and the matter of privileged communication, counselors need to be aware that:

    A. Privileged communication is present in every state in the Union for licensed professional counselors.
    B. Laws are unclear and may be different in different states.
    C. No clear laws govern this particular issue.
    D. State psychology laws are applicable here.

3. Which of the following is an example of a dual relationship?

    A. A counselor who provides counseling to their neighbor
    B. A counselor who works part-time as a bartender
    C. A counselor who hires a former client as an intern
    D. A counselor who is friends with a client's sibling

4. Which of the following is a requirement for obtaining informed consent?

    A. The counselor must provide a detailed diagnosis to the client
    B. The counselor must explain the potential risks and benefits of treatment
    C. The counselor must disclose all information shared by the client with a third party

D. The counselor must obtain written consent from the client's family members

5. Which of the following is an example of a boundary violation?

   A. A counselor who shares their personal problems with a client
   B. A counselor who refers a client to a specialist for additional treatment
   C. A counselor who charges a higher fee to clients who are more difficult to treat
   D. A counselor who attends a client's graduation ceremony as a supportive gesture

6. Which of the following is true regarding the use of touch in counseling?

   A. Touch should be avoided in all counseling settings
   B. Touch can be used as a form of therapy if the client consents
   C. Touch should only be used if the client initiates it
   D. Touch is only appropriate for certain cultural groups

7. Which of the following is true regarding the concept of confidentiality?

   A. Confidentiality can be broken if the counselor believes the client poses a threat to themselves or others
   B. Confidentiality can be broken if the counselor believes the client is not capable of making decisions
   C. Confidentiality can be broken if the counselor is required to do so by law
   D. All of the above

8. Which is NOT a potential ethical issue related to technology-assisted counseling?

   A. Informed consent
   B. Data privacy
   C. Appropriate use of social media
   D. Proper use of secure technology platforms

9. Which is NOT a recommended approach for addressing cultural differences in counseling?

    A. Encouraging the client to assimilate into the dominant culture
    B. Learning about the client's cultural background
    C. Recognizing and addressing one's own biases
    D. Adapting counseling techniques to fit the client's cultural background

10. Which is an example of a boundary crossing in counseling?

    A. Giving the client a ride home after a session
    B. Accepting a small gift from the client during the holidays
    C. Dating a former client after a reasonable amount of time has passed
    D. All of the above

11. Which is an example of a boundary violation in counseling?

    A. Offering advice outside the scope of one's training and expertise
    B. Maintaining appropriate physical distance from the client during sessions
    C. Refusing to provide services to a client based on personal beliefs or biases
    D. Using derogatory language or engaging in discriminatory behavior toward a client

12. Which is not an element of ethical decision-making in counseling?

    A. Recognizing the ethical dilemma
    B. Identifying possible courses of action
    C. Consulting with colleagues or supervisors
    D. Choosing the course of action that is most profitable

13. Among the following, which is NOT a recommended way to address potential ethical violations by a colleague?

    A. Directly confronting the colleague about the violation
    B. Reporting the violation to a supervisor or licensing board
    C. Ignoring the violation and continuing to work with the colleague

D. Seeking consultation from an ethics expert

14. Which of the situations would need a counselor to break confidentiality and warn a potential victim?

   A. A client reports feeling depressed
   B. A client discloses a plan to harm a specific individual
   C. A client discusses past drug use
   D. A client expresses anger toward a family member

15. The duty to warn clause:

   A. Requires counselors to report any criminal activity disclosed by a client
   B. Allows counselors to disclose confidential information to protect a client from harm
   C. Mandates that counselors report any suicidal ideation expressed by a client
   D. Requires counselors to disclose confidential information to prevent harm to a specific, identifiable person

16. The American Counseling Association (ACA) Code of Ethics:

   A. Provides guidelines for ethical and legal issues related to the practice of counseling
   B. Regulates the licensure of counselors in all states
   C. Establishes reimbursement rates for counseling services
   D. Mandates that all counseling sessions be recorded and made available to clients upon request

17. The purpose of state licensure laws for professional counselors is to:

   A. Ensure that counselors have the necessary training and qualifications to provide services to clients
   B. Regulate reimbursement rates for counseling services
   C. Establish ethical standards for the counseling profession
   D. Limit the number of counselors in a given geographic area

18. Informed consent in the counseling relationship refers to:

    A. A counselor's obligation to maintain confidentiality with clients
    B. A client's agreement to participate in counseling and their understanding of the nature of counseling
    C. A counselor's ability to diagnose and treat mental health disorders
    D. A client's agreement to pay for counseling services

19. Which of the following is NOT a requirement of HIPAA (Health Insurance Portability and Accountability Act) privacy rule for counselors?

    A. Counselors must obtain written consent before sharing clients' protected health information (PHI)
    B. Counselors must provide clients with a notice of privacy practices
    C. Counselors must obtain a client's signature on a release of information form before sharing PHI
    D. Counselors must keep clients' PHI confidential and secure.

20. Which of the following is a requirement of the NBCC (National Board for Certified Counselors) code of ethics regarding cultural competence?

    A. Counselors must strive to increase their understanding of their own culture and the culture of their clients
    B. Counselors must only work with clients who share the same cultural background as them
    C. Counselors must make assumptions about clients' cultural beliefs and practices
    D. Counselors must not incorporate clients' cultural beliefs and practices into treatment

The next chapter will cover the second topic of the eight core areas, which is social and cultural diversity.

Answer Key

Q.	1	2	3	4	5	6	7	8	9	10
A.	A	B	C	B	A	B	D	D	A	B

Q.	11	12	13	14	15	16	17	18	19	20
A.	D	D	C	B	D	A	A	B	C	A

Chapter Four: Social and Cultural Diversity

As counselors, we have to work with clients from different walks of life and distinct cultural backgrounds. It is important that we understand their unique perspectives and experiences and respect their individual differences.

We will follow a term-wise approach in this chapter. Here, you will get important definitions and meanings of the core terms relevant to the second core area. Come back to go over them whenever you need to.

List Of Terms

1. **Social and Cultural Diversity**: This applies to understanding the cultural context of issues, relationships, and trends in multicultural society along with its components, including

    A. Multicultural and pluralistic trends that cover different concerns and characteristics that determine diverse groups
    B. Attitudes, understandings, beliefs, and an acculturative understanding of the self as well as culturally distinct clients
    C. Theories surrounding multicultural counseling, social justice, and identity development
    D. Individual, couple, group, family, and community-related strategies for advocating and working for diverse populations

    E. Developing cultural self-awareness, advocacy, social justice, and optimal wellness

    F. Eliminating prejudices, biases, and processes of discrimination and oppression

2. **Culture**: This is a human experience that is mediated by psychological, biological, political, and historical events at universal, group, and individual levels.

3. **Cultural encapsulation**: This refers to treating and evaluating from a dominant culture point of view. The term was coined in 1962 by C. Gilbert Wrenn to emphasize the natural inclination of counselors to get bound by time and culture and avoid change and differences resulting from cross-cultural exposures and developments in society.

4. **Multicultural counseling**: This is the integration of cultural identities with the process of counseling

5. **Multiculturalism**: The fourth counseling force, multicultural counseling has become increasingly important as the population becomes more diverse. Multiculturalism in counseling practice refers to recognizing and appreciating diversity and incorporating cultural considerations into the counseling process. This includes understanding and respecting clients' different values, beliefs, and experiences from diverse backgrounds, such as race, ethnicity, gender, sexual orientation, religion, age, and ability. A multicultural approach to counseling involves being aware of how these cultural factors may influence a client's worldview, experiences, and presenting concerns and using this understanding to tailor counseling interventions that are sensitive and relevant to the client's cultural context. It also involves actively reducing biases and discrimination in the counseling process.

6. **Cultural Identity**: This refers to belonging and attachment to a particular cultural group or community. It includes various aspects such as ethnicity, language, customs, beliefs, and values that shape a person's perception of the world and their own self. Cultural identity can be influenced by factors such as family, upbringing, religion, and societal norms. It is an important aspect of an individual's personal and social identity.

7. The first racial identity model, known as the **Cross's Nigrescence Model**, was developed by William Cross Jr. It is a framework for understanding the identity development of Black Americans. The model has since been

revised and expanded and has influenced the development of other racial and ethnic identity models.

8. **The Tripartite model** of multicultural counseling is hinged on knowledge, skills, and awareness.

9. **Etic** refers to viewing clients from a universal point of view.

10. **Emic** refers to viewing situations from the cultural perspective of a client.

11. Important points to remember in regard to **communication patterns** are that:

   A. Most theories are reliant on the spoken word
   B. Second-language speakers may be at a disadvantage
   C. 85% of all communication is non-verbal

12. **High-context communication** is heavily dependent on surroundings and leaves a lot unsaid.

13. **Low-context communication** is mostly verbal.

14. **Paralanguage** involves verbal cues other than words, including pitch, volume, tempo, sound prolongation, etc.

15. **Kinesics** is all about body movements, postures, and positions, including gaze, eye contact, touch, and facial expressions.

16. **Chronemics** refers to studying how people perceive and use time in communication. This includes how people interpret and value time, organize and structure it, and use time to communicate messages in different contexts. Examples of chronemic behavior include punctuality, waiting times, and using time-related language.

17. **Monochromatic time** refers to a cultural perspective on time that sees it as a finite resource divided into measurable segments, such as seconds, minutes, and hours. This view of time is prevalent in Western cultures and places a high value on punctuality, schedules, and meeting deadlines.

18. **Polychromatic time** is a concept that refers to a cultural orientation in which people tend to do many things simultaneously, focus on relationships and human interactions, and do not place as much importance on time schedules. It contrasts with monochromatic time, where individuals focus on one task at a time and prioritizes punctuality and adherence to schedules.

19. **Proxemics**: In proxemics, personal physical distance is referred to as the different zones of space around individuals. There are four types of zones:

- Intimate distance (up to 18 inches)
- Personal distance (up to four feet)
- Social distance (up to 12 feet)
- Public distance (12 feet or more)

These zones determine the level of physical closeness or distance appropriate for different types of interactions and relationships. The intimate distance zone is typically reserved for close family members, romantic partners, or close friends. In contrast, the social distance zone is used for more formal social interactions like job interviews or business meetings. The public distance zone is the farthest away and is used for public speaking or other formal presentations.

20. **Acculturation**: the process of adjusting to and adopting the cultural practices and values of a new or different culture.
21. **Assimilation model**: a one-way process where someone gives up their individual cultural identity to conform to the dominant culture
22. **Separation model**: refers to a cultural adaptation process where an individual separates from the dominant culture and maintains their own culture
23. **Integration model/ biculturalism**: someone identifies with their own and other cultures
24. **Marginalized model**: someone rejects the cultural customs and values of both their own and the dominant cultures
25. **Worldview**: refers to the concept someone has of their relationship with the larger world
26. **Locus of responsibility**: refers to what system will be accountable for what happens to someone
27. **Internal locus of responsibility**: An individual's success or failure is their own responsibility.
28. **External locus of responsibility**: The social environment and external system is accountable for what happens to someone within it.
29. **Locus of control**: the degree of control someone has over their environment
30. **Internal locus of control**: The consequences that happen are the result of individual actions.
31. **External locus of control**: The consequences that happen do so because of chance.
32. The **Worldview framework**, introduced by Kluckhohn and Strodtbeck in

1961, is a paradigm that defines how people from various cultures see and interact with the world. The framework outlines five fundamental issues that aid in explaining cultural variations in worldview:

A. What is the essence of human nature?
B. What is the connection between humans and nature?
C. What is the relationship between different humans?
D. What is the connection between humans and groups?
E. What is the connection between humans and time?

Individuals may communicate their cultural worldview by answering these questions, which are formed by their culture's values, beliefs, and rituals. The framework assists counselors in understanding cultural differences and lays the groundwork for culturally responsive therapy.

33. **Race** can have distinct meanings:

A. Physical characteristics, including facial features, color, and skin
B. Social and political classification on the basis of biology and genetics
C. Race according to a census that most identify with

34. **Color consciousness**: describes a heightened awareness or sensitivity to race and ethnicity in interpersonal and societal interactions. It is often associated with a critical examination of power dynamics related to race and the impacts of systemic racism on marginalized communities. Color consciousness differs from color blindness, which emphasizes a disregard for racial differences in favor of treating everyone as individuals.

35. **Colorism**: a form of racism where worth is attached on the basis of how closely someone else's skin approximates that of whites.

36. **Biracial**: someone who belongs to two different races biologically.

37. **Mulatto**: someone of mixed heritage, with one parent being black and the other being white. The term is offensive.

38. **Mestizo** is a Latin American term to describe people with mixed European and Indigenous American ancestry. The term originated during the Spanish colonial period and denotes people of mixed racial heritage in Latin American countries.

39. **Eugenics movement**: The eugenics movement aspired to enhance the

human race by selecting breeding people with desired features and preventing those considered "undesirable" from reproducing.

40. **Ethnicity:** people who identify with a group depending on similar social and cultural backgrounds

41. **Ethnocentrism:** a dominant cultural group that believes it is superior to others

42. **Socioeconomic class or status:** highlights the different views of the world, problems, the self, and essential needs that must be met.

43. **Classism:** refers to a form of discrimination

44. **Structural classism:** promotes the existing status quo

45. **Internalized classism:** leads to people feeling ashamed because of the class they belong to.

46. **Gender:** The socially created roles, attitudes, and expectations linked to being male or female are referred to as gender. It encompasses how people identify, express themselves, and interact with others following cultural and social standards. Gender is not identical to biological sex, which is defined by a person's physical traits at birth.

47. **Gender schema theory** proposes that children develop mental categories of gender that influence their understanding and behavior in society.

48. **Sexual orientation** has four components: physical identity (biological), gender identity (beliefs about your gender), social sexual roles (roles that are adopted by the prevailing culture), and sexual orientation (emotions and attraction in relation to sex).

49. **Questioning** can refer to someone who is unsure about their sexual identity

50. **Affectional orientation** is an attraction hinged on emotional stability, intelligence, communication patterns, and other interpersonal elements.

51. **Heterosexism** is the belief that heterosexuality is the only normal and natural sexual orientation and that other orientations are inferior or abnormal.

52. **Homophobia** refers to the tendency of some people to be afraid of and hate sexual minorities

53. **Internalized homophobia** refers to the negative attitudes, beliefs, and feelings towards oneself based on their perceived or actual LGBTQ+ identity, which can result from societal stigma and discrimination. It can lead to self-hatred, shame, and a negative self-concept.

54. **Homoprejudice** refers to the negative attitudes, beliefs, and stereotypes towards people who identify as gay, lesbian, bisexual, or transgender.

55. **Buddhism** is a religion based on the teachings of the Buddha. The goal is to increase awareness and understanding of the deeper realities of life to reduce anxiety and achieve nirvana.

56. **Confucianism** is an East Asian ethical and philosophical system that emphasizes the completion of a person through moral, cognitive, and educational goals, harmonious and humble relationships, family, tranquility, and the practice of li (ritual propriety).

57. **Hinduism** is a belief system based on the idea of a universal spirit (Brahman) with reincarnation and karma governing one's destiny.

58. **Islam** is a monotheistic religion founded by Prophet Muhammad. It propagates faith in one God, Allah, and the importance of following the teachings in the Quran. The religion emphasizes prayer, sharing wealth, forgiveness, benevolence, fasting, and spiritual pilgrimage to Mecca. Muslims also believe in the prophets of Judaism and Christianity, including Abraham and the first five books of the Old Testament.

59. **Judaism** is a monotheistic religion. It emphasizes performing good deeds, following the Torah, and studying Kabbalah. Jews believe in interacting positively with others, performing mitzvot, and making ethical choices throughout life.

60. **Taoism** emphasizes living in harmony with nature, seeking inner peace, and recognizing the power of the Dao. Its focus includes reality, human life, and the universe. It advocates for intense study and enlightenment. All people are believed to have a moral center.

61. **Agnosticism** is the belief that the existence of the ultimate truth and a higher power is unknowable.

62. **Atheism** is disbelief in the existence of a divine force, aka God.

63. **Ableism** is discrimination and prejudice against individuals with disabilities, including the assumption of their inferiority and exclusion from society.

64. **The Rehabilitation Act of 1973** is a U.S. law that prohibits discrimination against individuals with disabilities in federal programs and activities. It also established the Rehabilitation Services Administration, which provides vocational rehabilitation services and support for people with disabilities to achieve employment and independent living.

65. **The Americans with Disabilities Act** is an act that stops discrimination against disabled individuals. It requires employers and other covered entities to reasonably accomodate individuals with disabilities, such as

modifications to facilities, policies, or procedures, to ensure equal access and opportunity. The ADA has been amended several times to clarify its scope and strengthen its protections.

66. **Equity** refers to a balanced allocation of rights, services and duties in society.

67. **Access** is all about fair access to services and adherence to the Bill of Rights.

68. **Oppression** is depriving someone else by force and also includes racism, classism and ableism.

69. **Primary oppression** is obvious acts of deprivation and force.

70. **Secondary oppression** covers oppressive acts where the perpetrator is indirectly involved.

71. **Tertiary oppression** is when minority groups accept the majority opinion to fit in. This can lead to PTSD.

72. **Antilocution** is sharing harmful views with those with the same beliefs.

73. **Avoidance** happens when someone purposefully avoids interacting with those they do not appreciate.

74. **Discrimination** happens when someone is denied access to resources.

75. **Physical attack** has overtly violent or violent undertones and happens in high-pressure situations or against a target group.

76. **Extermination** is a forced effort to demolish certain social groups and people.

77. **Racism** has two types: covert (not obvious) and overt (obvious). It can happen at individual, group, and institutional levels.

78. **Resilience** is the ability to maintain balance and adjust to changing circumstances. It is hinged on hope, a good support network, and a sense of safety around one's community.

79. Dr. Pamela Hays established the **Hays model** in 1996, which outlines six phases of cultural identity development that people may go through as they get a better awareness of their cultural identity and how it impacts their experiences and worldview. The **Gray model**, created by psychologist Dr. William E. Cross Jr. in 1971 and later extended by Na'im Akbar in 1991, focuses on how black identities are formed in the states. Both of these theories are valuable for comprehending the complicated process of cultural identity formation and how it influences a person's ideas, feelings, and behaviors.

80. The **racial identity development model** for people of color has five stages:

    A. Pre-encounter: Before experiencing a racial event, individuals may be unaware of the impact of race on their lives.
    B. Encounter: After a specific experience of racial discrimination or prejudice, individuals may start to question their racial identity and how it affects them.
    C. Immersion-Emersion: In response to conflicts related to race, individuals may seek out more information about their own racial group and may feel anger or frustration towards other groups.
    D. Internalization: Individuals become more accepting of their racial identity and learn to integrate it with other cultural identities they have.
    E. Internalization-commitment: Individuals become advocates for their racial group and work towards improving social justice and equality for all people of color.

Questions and Answers

1. Which term describes the unequal treatment of individuals based on their group membership?

    A. Stereotyping
    B. Prejudice
    C. Discrimination
    D. Racism

2. What is the term for the idea that one's own cultural group is superior to others?

    A. Stereotyping
    B. Prejudice
    C. Discrimination
    D. Ethnocentrism

3. Which term describes the process of adapting to and incorporating elements of a new culture?

    A. Assimilation
    B. Integration
    C. Multiculturalism
    D. Acculturation

4. Which term describes the ability to function effectively in a multicultural environment?

    A. Cultural awareness
    B. Cultural sensitivity
    C. Cultural competence
    D. Cultural humility

5. What is the term for the characteristics that define a cultural group?

    A. Prejudice

B. Stereotype

C. Culture

D. Race

6. What is the term for identifying and challenging one's own cultural biases and assumptions?

    A. Cultural competence

    B. Cultural humility

    C. Cultural awareness

    D. Cultural sensitivity

7. Which term describes the process of creating a shared culture among different cultural groups?

    A. Assimilation

    B. Integration

    C. Multiculturalism

    D. Acculturation

8. Which term describes a group's unique way of life, including shared beliefs, values, customs, behaviors, and artifacts?

    A. Stereotype

    B. Prejudice

    C. Culture

    D. Race

9. Which term describes the tendency to view people and events through the lens of one's own cultural background?

    A. Stereotyping

    B. Prejudice

    C. Discrimination

    D. Cultural bias

10. Which term describes the belief that all members of a group share the same characteristics and behaviors?

    A. Stereotyping
    B. Prejudice
    C. Discrimination
    D. Racism

11. What is the term for the social, economic, and political disadvantage experienced by individuals based on their group membership?

    A. Stereotyping
    B. Prejudice
    C. Oppression
    D. Discrimination

12. Which term describes the process of recognizing and respecting the differences among cultures?

    A. Cultural awareness
    B. Cultural sensitivity
    C. Cultural competence
    D. Cultural humility

13. Which term describes the tendency to see one's own culture as the norm and judge others based on that standard?

    A. Stereotyping
    B. Prejudice
    C. Ethnocentrism
    D. Discrimination

14. What is the term for the expectations and assumptions based on an individual's group membership?

    A. Prejudice
    B. Stereotype
    C. Culture

D. Race

15. Which term describes the process of actively valuing and respecting diversity among individuals and groups?

   A. Multiculturalism
   B. Integration
   C. Assimilation
   D. Acculturation

16. What is the term for identifying and examining power and privilege in society?

   A. Social justice
   B. Oppression
   C. Activism
   D. Equity

17. Which term describes the idea that race and ethnicity intersect with other aspects of identity to create unique experiences of oppression and privilege?

   A. Intersectionality
   B. Stereotyping
   C. Prejudice
   D. Discrimination

18. What is the term to denote the set of behaviors and attitudes that allow individuals to effectively navigate different cultural environments?

   A. Cultural awareness
   B. Cultural sensitivity
   C. Cultural competence
   D. Cultural humility

19. Which term describes the process of adapting to and incorporating elements of a new culture while also maintaining one's own cultural identity?

   A. Assimilation

B. Integration
C. Multiculturalism
D. Biculturalism

20. Which term describes the conscious and deliberate effort to create a more equitable society by challenging systems of power and privilege?

A. Social justice
B. Oppression
C. Activism
D. Equity

In the next chapter, we will cover the third core area that spans human growth and development.

Answer Key

Q.	1	2	3	4	5	6	7	8	9	10
A.	C	D	D	C	C	B	B	C	D	A

Q.	11	12	13	14	15	16	17	18	19	20
A.	C	B	C	B	A	A	A	C	D	C

Chapter Five: Human Growth and Development

Human growth and development is a multidisciplinary domain drawing from sociology, biology, psychology, and related fields. This core area is all about what makes human beings who we are, how we develop from infancy to adulthood, and the different factors that influence our belief systems, personalities and values along the way. Let us now look at each of the important areas under this core topic.

Foundational Issues

Foundational issues lie at the base of any important topic. These are some essential ones to consider regarding human growth and development.

1. Nature vs. Nurture: This issue refers to the debate regarding the relative contributions of genetic and environmental factors in shaping human development. Some theorists argue that genetic factors have a greater influence, while others argue that environmental factors are more important (MedicineNet, 2019). Most researchers now recognize that nature and nurture play a role in shaping human development.

2. Continuity vs. Discontinuity: This analyzes whether development occurs gradually and continuously over time or whether it occurs in distinct stages. Some theorists argue that development is a continuous process, while others argue that it occurs in distinct stages with sudden and dramatic changes.

3. Stability vs. Change: This questions whether human traits and characteristics are stable and unchanging over time or can change and be influenced by experience. Some theorists argue that human traits are largely stable and unchanging, while others argue that they are more malleable and subject to change.
4. Active vs. Passive: This is related to the debate about whether humans are active agents who shape their development or passive recipients of environmental influences. Some theorists argue that humans actively shape their own development, while others argue that environmental factors have a greater influence.
5. Universality vs. Context Specificity: This discusses whether human development is a universal process that is the same across all cultures and contexts or whether cultural and contextual factors shape it.

Knowing these foundational issues helps counselors comprehensively understand human development's complex processes.

Special designs in HGD research

The first special design is **case studies**. These can be used in different fields, including psychology, to learn everything possible about a specific group of people or an individual and then generalize this information to an extended population.

Then there are **naturalistic studies**. These are observational studies where you look at your research subjects in their own environments. The purpose is to explore their behaviors without external control or influence. This research method is used in field studies.

Survey research is a type of study that involves collecting data from a sample of individuals through standardized questionnaires or interviews. This method is commonly used in social sciences to study attitudes, opinions, behaviors, and other variables of interest among a specific population.

Correlational research studies examine the relationship between two or more variables. They aim to determine if a relationship exists between variables and, if so, to what extent. This method is commonly used in social sciences to study the association between different factors or variables.

In **cross-sectional studies**, researchers collect data from a sample of individuals at a single point in time to investigate a particular phenomenon or to determine the prevalence of a particular characteristic or behavior within a population.

Longitudinal studies involve gathering data from the same group of individuals over an extended period, allowing researchers to investigate changes in a particular phenomenon or relationship over time. This approach can help identify patterns of development or change in variables of interest.

Time-lag studies necessitate data collection at different points in time from different groups of individuals to investigate changes over time in a particular phenomenon or relationship. This approach can help identify causal relationships between variables by establishing the timing of their occurrence.

The central nervous system (CNS)

The human central nervous system is a vital component of our biological makeup. It plays an irreplaceable role in coordinating and regulating various bodily function s. Our spinal cords and brains together form the central nervous system, and they are interconnected and function together to facilitate communication and control throughout the body (Vandergriendt, 2022).

The brain, the command center of the CNS, is responsible for processing and interpreting information received from the body and external environment. It is divided into several regions, each specializing in different functions.

The brain's outermost layer forms the cerebral cortex. This is associated with higher cognitive functions such as perception, memory, language, and problem-solving.

The limbic system, located deeper within the brain, plays a pivotal role in regulating emotions, motivation, and memory formation.

The brainstem bridges the brain and the spinal cord and supervises basic life-sustaining functions like breathing, heart rate, and digestion.

The spinal cord forges a bridge between our brains and peripheral nervous systems (PNS). It is responsible for distributing information between a complex network of nerves (Vandergriendt, 2022). It also plays a role in reflex actions, rapidly coordinating responses to sensory stimuli without involving the brain. This ability ensures swift reactions to potential dangers or harmful stimuli.

Neurons, the fundamental building blocks of the CNS, are specialized cells that transmit electrical signals. They are threefold and comprise a cell body, dendrites, and an axon. Dendrites get incoming signals from other neurons, while axons transmit outgoing signals to other neurons or effector cells. The transmission of signals between neurons occurs through synapses, which are small gaps where chemical neurotransmitters facilitate the passage of information (National Institute of Neurological Disorders and Stroke, 2022).

Various factors, including genetics, environmental stimuli, and experiences, influence our central nervous systems. Imbalances within the CNS can lead to anxiety, depression, and schizophrenia, among other mental health concerns. Consequently, understanding the CNS is crucial for counselors, as it provides insights into the biological underpinnings of these conditions and informs therapeutic interventions.

The brain

The human brain is an incredibly remarkable organ that acts as the command center of the central nervous system (CNS). It is responsible for controlling and coordinating various bodily functions, as well as enabling our thoughts, emotions, and behaviors. The brain is divided into distinct regions, each with specific functions (Hirsch, 2018). The outermost cerebral cortex plays a crucial role in higher cognitive functions such as perception, attention, memory, language, and problem-solving. It is divided into different lobes, including the frontal, parietal, temporal, and occipital lobes, each responsible for various sensory and cognitive processes (The University of Queensland, 2018).

Deep within the brain lies the limbic system, which regulates emotions, motivation, and memory. It includes structures like the amygdala, hippocampus, and hypothalamus (RajMohan & Mohandas, 2007). The amygdala is associated with processing emotions and fear responses, while the hippocampus plays a vital role in forming and consolidating memories. The hypothalamus helps regulate basic physiological functions like hunger, thirst, sleep, and body temperature.

The brainstem serves as a connector between the brain and the spinal cord. It is responsible for controlling essential life-sustaining functions, including breathing, heart rate, and digestion. Additionally, it serves as a pathway for motor and sensory signs from the brain to the remainder of our bodies.

Neurons, the building blocks of the brain, are specialized cells that transmit electrical signals. The brain is home to billions of neurons interconnected through intricate networks. These neurons communicate with each other through synapses, small gaps where chemical neurotransmitters facilitate the transmission of information.

The human brain is very adaptable and capable of change throughout life. This phenomenon, known as neuroplasticity, allows the brain to reorganize its get-up and function in accordance with new experiences, learning, and rehabilitation after injury (Puderbaugh & Emmady, 2022). By staying abreast of advancements in neuroscience and integrating this knowledge into their practice, counselors can better support their clients and tailor interventions that promote positive mental health and well-being.

Genetic disorders

Genetic disorders are a diverse group of conditions arising from abnormalities or mutations in an individual's genetic material. They can affect various aspects of human health and development, and understanding genetic disorders is essential for healthcare professionals and individuals preparing for the National Counselor Examination (NCE).

Genes contain instructions for building and maintaining the body. Genetic disorders can occur when there are changes or mutations in the genes. These mutations can be inherited or arise spontaneously during an individual's lifetime

(Medline Plus, 2020). There are different types of genetic disorders, including single-gene, chromosomal, and multifactorial disorders. Mutations in a specific gene cause single-gene disorders. They can be classified into two types: dominant and recessive. Dominant disorders occur when a mutation is present in one gene, while recessive disorders require both gene copies to be mutated. Single-gene disorders include cystic fibrosis, Huntington's disease, and sickle cell anemia (Genetic Alliance & District of Columbia Department of Health, 2010).

Chromosomal disorders occur when there are changes in the structure or number of chromosomes. Down syndrome, for instance, occurs due to the prevalence of an extra copy of chromosome 21 (CDC, 2021). Other examples include Turner syndrome, characterized by the absence of one X chromosome in females, and Klinefelter syndrome, characterized by an extra X chromosome in males. Multifactorial disorders are the result of genetic and environmental factors. They result from the interaction between multiple genes and environmental influences (Medline Plus, 2021). Examples of multifactorial disorders include heart disease, diabetes, and some types of cancer. Lifestyle choices and genetic predispositions can influence these disorders.

Genetic counseling has a key role in understanding and managing genetic disorders. Genetic counselors provide information and support to individuals and families who stand to be impacted (or are already impacted) by genetic disorders. They help assess the risk of inheriting or passing on a genetic condition, explain available testing options, and guides for making informed decisions about family planning and healthcare.

Classical conditioning

Classical conditioning is a fundamental concept in behavioral psychology that explains how associations between stimuli can lead to learned behaviors. It involves pairing a neutral stimulus with an unconditioned stimulus to elicit a response (Cherry, 2023). The neutral stimulus ultimately becomes a conditioned stimulus that can trigger a conditioned response. This process was famously demonstrated by Ivan Pavlov's experiments with dogs, where he associated a bell (neutral stimulus) with food (unconditioned stimulus) to elicit salivation (unconditioned response). Classical conditioning is crucial in understanding and modifying behaviors and has practical applications in various fields, including therapy and education.

Operant conditioning

Operant conditioning is a concept in behavioral psychology that focuses on how behaviors are influenced by their consequences. It involves the association between a behavior and its consequence, which can either reinforce or diminish the propensity of that behavior repeating itself (Staddon & Cerutti, 2002). Through operant conditioning, behaviors can be shaped, modified, or extinguished. Reinforcement involves providing a positive consequence to increase the likelihood of behavior, while punishment involves providing a negative consequence to decrease the likelihood. This type of conditioning, pioneered by B.F. Skinner, is widely used in various settings, such as education, therapy, and behavior management, to shape desired behaviors and reduce unwanted ones.

Social learning

Social learning is a theory in psychology that emphasizes the importance of observational learning and modeling behaviors through social interactions. According to social learning theory, individuals learn by observing others and imitating their actions, attitudes, and behaviors. This process involves attention, retention, reproduction, and motivation (Fitzgibbons, 2019). Observing others allows individuals to acquire new knowledge, skills, and behaviors without direct personal experience. Role models and social influences play a significant role in shaping behavior and attitudes. Social learning theory has practical implications in fields such as education, therapy, and behavior change, as it highlights the impact of social interactions and provides insights into how behaviors can be learned and modified through observation and modeling.

The Dollard and Miller approach

The Dollard and Miller approach, also known as the social learning theory of personality, was developed by John Dollard and Neal Miller in 1950. This approach emphasizes the role of learning and social factors in shaping personality and behavior (Niwlikar, 2021). According to Dollard and Miller, behavior is influenced by a combination of drives, cues, responses, and rewards. They proposed that individuals learn through imitation and reinforcement, where they observe and imitate the behaviors of others and are motivated by the positive or negative repercussions of those behaviors. The Dollard and Miller approach highlights the importance of environmental factors and social learning in understanding human behavior and personality development.

Cognitive development

Cognitive development refers to the process by which an individual acquires knowledge, thinking abilities, problem-solving skills, and understanding of the world. It encompasses the development of perception, attention, memory, language, reasoning, and problem-solving skills. The study of cognitive development gained prominence through the pioneering work of Jean Piaget, who proposed a stage theory of cognitive development. According to Piaget, children progress through distinct stages, each characterized by specific cognitive abilities and ways of thinking (Cherry, 2022). Genetic factors, environmental experiences, and social interactions influence cognitive development.

Lev Vygotsky's cognitive development theory

Lev Vygotsky's cognitive development theory, introduced in the early 20th century, emphasizes the role of social interactions and cultural influences in shaping cognitive development. According to Vygotsky, learning is a collaborative process through social interactions and scaffolding (Mcleod, 2023). He proposed that individuals acquire knowledge and develop cognitive abilities through interactions with more knowledgeable others, such as parents, teachers, or peers. Vygotsky highlighted the importance of the Zone of Proximal Development (ZPD), which refers to the gap between an individual's current level of ability and their potential level with assistance. The ZPD represents the optimal range for learning, as learners receive support to master tasks and gradually internalize their knowledge and skills. Vygotsky's cognitive development theory emphasizes the social and cultural aspects of learning, highlighting the significance of social interactions, language, and cultural context in cognitive development.

Cognition and memory

Cognition and memory are closely intertwined aspects of human mental processes. Cognition refers to mental activities such as acquiring, processing, and using information. It encompasses perception, attention, language, problem-solving, and decision-making. On the other hand, memory is the capacity to encode, store, and retrieve information. It involves the processes of encoding (acquiring information), storage (retaining information), and retrieval (recalling information). Memory is crucial for learning, allowing us to retain and recall previously learned knowledge and experiences. Cognition and memory are interconnected, as cognitive processes influence how information is encoded and retrieved, while memory enables cognitive functions and supports our ability to think, reason, and problem-solve.

Other important concepts in cognitive development

1. Vygotsky proposed three stages in speech development:

    A. Social Speech, where children communicate through social interactions.
    B. Egocentric Speech, characterized by self-directed speech.
    C. Inner Speech, internalized thoughts used for problem-solving.

These stages highlight the role of social interactions and language in cognitive development.

2. Elementary mental functions are those for which no additional thought or learning is needed.
3. Vygotsky's sociocultural theory emphasizes the role of scaffolding and social interaction in cognitive development. Scaffolding involves providing temporary support and guidance to learners within their Zone of Proximal Development, enabling them to accomplish tasks beyond their current

abilities. Social interaction provides the necessary context for learning, as individuals learn from more knowledgeable others through collaboration, instruction, and shared experiences.

4. Piaget's stages of cognitive development include the Sensorimotor stage (0-2 years), Preoperational stage (2-7 years), Concrete Operational stage (7-11 years), and Formal Operational stage (11 years and beyond). These stages represent the progressive development of cognitive abilities, such as object permanence, symbolic thinking, concrete reasoning, and abstract thinking, throughout childhood and adolescence.

5. According to nativists, a critical development period is a specific time window during which certain skills or abilities must be acquired for optimal development. If these skills are not acquired within the critical period, acquiring them later in life becomes much more difficult or even impossible (Litchfield & Lambert, 2011).

6. The nativist approach posits that certain aspects of knowledge and behavior are innate and biologically determined. It emphasizes the role of genetics and the existence of pre-existing structures or mechanisms that guide development. Nativists believe these innate factors interact with the environment to shape cognitive and linguistic development.

7. The smallest combination of sounds that are meaningful is known as morpheme.

8. Freud's stages of psychosexual development include the Oral stage (0-1 year), Anal stage (1-3 years), Phallic stage (3-6 years), Latency stage (6-12 years), and Genital stage (puberty onwards). These stages represent the progression of libido-focused pleasure and conflicts associated with different erogenous zones, influencing personality development and psychosexual behavior (Mcleod, 2019).

Personality development

Personality development is the ongoing process through which an individual's unique thoughts, emotions, and behaviors are shaped and expressed. A combination of genetic, environmental, and social factors influences it. Personality development encompasses various psychodynamic, behavioral, cognitive, and humanistic approaches. These highlight different aspects, such as unconscious processes, learning experiences, cognitive processes, and self-actualization, that contribute to developing personality traits, values, beliefs, and overall psychological well-being. Personality development continues throughout life, influenced by life experiences, relationships, and personal growth efforts, as individuals strive to achieve a sense of identity, coherence, and self-fulfillment.

Questions and Answers

This section of questions and answers will cover important points of the core area of human growth and development. Finish it before moving to the next segment.

1. Which is NOT considered a prenatal development stage?

   A. Germinal stage
   B. Embryonic stage
   C. Fetal stage
   D. Neonatal stage

2. The ability to mentally represent objects that are not present is known as:

   A. Object permanence
   B. Conservation
   C. Egocentrism
   D. Abstract thinking

3. According to Erik Erikson, the major psychosocial crisis during adolescence is:

   A. Identity vs. Role Confusion
   B. Trust vs. Mistrust
   C. Autonomy vs. Shame and Doubt
   D. Integrity vs. Despair

4. The process of developing schemas by incorporating new information into existing schemas is called:

   A. Assimilation
   B. Accommodation
   C. Equilibration
   D. Object permanence

5. According to Lawrence Kohlberg, the highest level of moral development is:

   A. Preconventional
   B. Conventional

    C. Postconventional
    D. Egocentric

6. Which is NOT a component of Albert Bandura's social-cognitive theory?

    A. Observational learning
    B. Self-efficacy
    C. Self-esteem
    D. Reciprocal determinism

7. The ability to consider other's perspectives and understand their thoughts and feelings is called:

    A. Theory of Mind
    B. Conservation
    C. Egocentrism
    D. Object permanence

8. According to Jean Piaget, children in the concrete operational stage can understand:

    A. Abstract reasoning
    B. Cause-and-effect relationships
    C. Conservation
    D. All of the above

9. Which of the following is NOT a psychosocial crisis in Erik Erikson's theory?

    A. Intimacy vs. Isolation
    B. Industry vs. Inferiority
    C. Generativity vs. Stagnation
    D. Egocentrism vs. Altruism

10. According to Freud's psychosexual theory, the focus of pleasure during the phallic stage is on which body part?

    A. Mouth
    B. Genitals

C. Anal region

D. None of the above

11. Which developmental psychologist is known for his work on moral reasoning?

    A. Erik Erikson

    B. Lawrence Kohlberg

    C. Lev Vygotsky

    D. Jean Piaget

12. The period of rapid physical and sexual maturation during adolescence is called:

    A. Menopause

    B. Andropause

    C. Puberty

    D. Midlife crisis

13. Which theory emphasizes the influence of sociocultural factors on development?

    A. Psychodynamic theory

    B. Behaviorist theory

    C. Social-cognitive theory

    D. Sociocultural theory

14. The attachment style characterized by a lack of trust in others and a fear of rejection is called:

    A. Secure attachment

    B. Avoidant attachment

    C. Ambivalent attachment

    D. Disorganized attachment

15. According to Abraham Maslow's hierarchy of needs, which needs must be met first before progressing to higher-level needs?

    A. Physiological needs
    B. Safety needs
    C. Belongingness and love needs
    D. Self-esteem needs

16. The cognitive development stage during which children acquire the ability to mentally represent objects through symbols is called:

    A. Sensorimotor stage
    B. Preoperational stage
    C. Concrete operational stage
    D. Formal operational stage

17. The process of aging that involves a decline in cognitive abilities, such as problem-solving and memory, is called:

    A. Dementia
    B. Alzheimer's disease
    C. Senescence
    D. Cognitive impairment

18. According to Erik Erikson, the primary developmental task during early adulthood is:

    A. Identity formation
    B. Intimacy
    C. Generativity
    D. Integrity

19. The theory that emphasizes the role of rewards and punishments in shaping behavior is:

    A. Psychodynamic theory
    B. Behaviorist theory

C. Cognitive theory
D. Humanistic theory

20. The process of refining and organizing information in memory to enhance retrieval is known as:

A. Encoding
B. Storage
C. Retrieval
D. Consolidation

In the next chapter, we will move on to the career development aspect of the NCE syllabus.

Answer Key

Q.	1	2	3	4	5	6	7	8	9	10
A.	D	A	A	A	C	C	A	D	D	B

Q.	11	12	13	14	15	16	17	18	19	20
A.	B	C	D	B	A	B	C	B	B	D

Chapter Six: Career Development

The career development section of the core NCE topics focuses on assisting individuals in identifying and pursuing their professional goals. It offers guidance on career planning, job search strategies, resume and interview preparation, networking, and continuous professional growth, enabling them to navigate and thrive in their chosen career paths. In this chapter, we will cover important keywords that could feature as part of your exam questions. You can find more such crucial keypoints at quizlet.com!

Important Terms

1. Approximately 61% of married couple families in the United States are two-income families where both spouses are working.
2. One out of every five job applicants can get a job purely based on chance.
3. Re-entry women: Refers to women who have taken a break from the professional front and are now seeking to re-enter the workforce. They often face unique challenges and require support to transition smoothly back into professional life.
4. Displaced homemaker: Describes individuals, typically women, who have lost their primary source of income and role because of factors like divorce, separation, or the death of a spouse. They often need assistance in acquiring new skills and finding employment.

5. Glass ceiling: This represents an invisible barrier that limits the advancement of certain groups, particularly women and minorities, within organizations. It refers to the barriers and biases that prevent these individuals from reaching higher levels of leadership and success.

6. Victor Vroom's Motivation and Management Expectancy Theory: Developed by psychologist Victor Vroom, this theory explains how people's motivation to perform a task is influenced by their expectations of the outcome and the perceived value they place on that outcome. It emphasizes the importance of individual beliefs and preferences in determining motivation.

7. Vocational guidance: Refers to the process of providing individuals with information, resources, and support to aid them in making informed choices about their career paths. It involves assessing their interests, skills, and aptitudes to guide them toward suitable vocational options.

8. Career counseling: Involves providing professional guidance and support to individuals in making career-related decisions, managing career transitions, and developing necessary skills for career success. It helps individuals explore their interests, values, and goals to create a fulfilling and satisfying career path.

9. Avocation: Refers to a hobby or passion pursued alongside one's primary occupation. It represents activities that individuals engage in for personal enjoyment, self-expression, or relaxation, often without seeking financial gain or making it their primary career focus.

10. Dual-career families: Refers to households in which both partners pursue professional careers concurrently. These families often face unique challenges in balancing work and personal life, requiring effective communication, shared responsibilities, and support systems to maintain career satisfaction and family harmony.

11. Title VII, Civil Rights Act: A landmark federal law prohibiting employment prejudice and discrimination based on race, color, religion, sex, or national origin. It provides protection and promotes equal opportunities in hiring, promotion, and workplace practices.

12. 80% Four-fifths Rule: A guideline used in employment discrimination law to assess the potential adverse impact on protected groups. If a group's selection rate is lower than 80% of that of the group which has the highest rate, it may indicate discriminatory practices.

13. Adverse impact: Refers to the unintentional discriminatory effect of employment practices or policies that disproportionately impact protected groups. It occurs when a seemingly neutral practice results in a substantial difference in employment outcomes for different groups.

14. Differential validity: Relates how a selection procedure or test predicts job performance differently for different groups. It focuses on evaluating whether a test or assessment exhibits fairness and validity across diverse populations.

15. Trait-and-factor theory: A career development theory that emphasizes the match between an individual's personal traits, abilities, and interests with the requirements of a specific occupation. It suggests that career choice and success are influenced by aligning personal attributes with job demands.

16. Profile matching: Involves comparing an individual's personal characteristics, such as skills, interests, and values, with the requirements of various occupations. It aims to identify career options that align with an individual's profile, facilitating informed decision-making.

17. Trait-and-factor model: An approach to career counseling based on the trait-and-factor theory. It involves assessing an individual's traits, such as aptitudes and interests, and then matching them with the characteristics of suitable occupations to guide career decision-making.

18. Parsons' three steps to implement trait-and-factor model: Developed by psychologist Frank Parsons, the three steps involve understanding oneself (assessing skills, interests, and values), exploring the world of work (researching occupations), and integrating the two to make an informed career decision.

19. Developmental approaches (to career counseling): Focus on understanding the individual's career development throughout their lifespan. These approaches consider personal growth, life roles, and transitions, aiming to help individuals explore and align their careers with their evolving needs, values, and circumstances.

20. Frank Parsons is the father of vocational guidance.

21. Edmund Griffith Williamson was the chief spokesperson for the Minnesota Viewpoint. This was a group that delved deeper into Parsons' career counseling model and supposedly used Minnestoa Occupational Rating Scales.

22. Middle-class and upper-middle-class white males without disabilities form the basis of most well-known career theories.

23. Frank Parsons wrote *Choosing A Vocation* in 1909.
24. Important points on Anne Roe:

    A. Suggested a career approach based on personality. The premise was that a career exists to satisfy some form of unconscious need.
    B. Proposed needs that get satisfied are not unconscious motivators.
    C. Higher order needs may disappear even if they are never met, but the ones that are lower order, like safety, will always be of primary concern.
    D. Needs that get satisfied after long periods serve as unconscious motivating factors.
    E. Anne Roe was the first career specialist who employed a two-dimensional system related to occupational classification, where she considered both fields and levels.
    F. Roe's eight occupational fields were business contract, technology, organizations, science, general culture, outdoor, arts and entertainment, and service.
    G. Her six levels of occupational skill were professional and managerial 1 and 2, semiprofessional and small businesses, skilled, semi-skilled, and unskilled.

25. Edwin Bordin relied on the premise of the unconscious mind to analyze career choices.
26. John Holland's work is the most popular approach for career choices. He developed the self-directed search (SDS) for measuring the six personality types. The types are social, artistic, investigative, realistic, enterprising, and conventional.
27. According to Ginzberg and colleagues, career choice development involves three key aspects. Firstly, it is an ongoing process that spans throughout an individual's life. Secondly, career decisions are made continuously throughout one's life. Lastly, once a career choice is made, it is seen as a permanent decision that cannot be easily reversed.
28. Donald Super emphasized the self-concept. This emphasizes that individuals' career choices are influenced by their evolving self-concept, which includes factors like interests, abilities, values, and personality, shaping their vocational development. To him, the five stages of career development are

growth (birth to 14 years), exploration (15 to 24 years), establishment (22 to 44 years), maintenance (44 to 64 years), and decline (after 65 years).

29. Gelatt Decision Model: Gelatt's decision model emphasizes the importance of information and the role of uncertainty in career decision-making, highlighting the need to gather and evaluate information systematically.

30. Occupational Outlook Handbook (OOH): The OOH is a comprehensive resource published by the U.S. Bureau of Labor Statistics, providing detailed information on various occupations, including job duties, education requirements, salary data, and future employment prospects.

31. Underemployment: Underemployment refers to a situation where individuals are employed in careers that fall below their qualifications, skills, or experience, leading to a mismatch between their capabilities and the demands of their current work.

32. Guide for Occupational Exploration (GOE): The GOE is a resource that offers career information and descriptions of various occupations, helping individuals explore and gain insights into different career paths, requirements, and opportunities.

33. Contrast effect: The contrast effect refers to the phenomenon where individuals evaluate or perceive something differently based on a recent or preceding comparison, influencing their judgment and perception of certain qualities or attributes.

34. Compensatory effect: The compensatory effect suggests that individuals may prioritize or emphasize certain factors or qualities in decision-making to compensate for perceived shortcomings in other areas, aiming to balance and fulfill their overall needs or desires.

35. Strong Interest Inventory (SCII): The SCII is a widely used career assessment tool that measures individuals' interests across different occupational areas, providing insights into potential career paths and helping individuals align their interests with suitable occupations.

36. Kuder Occupational Interest Survey (KOIS): The KOIS is an interest inventory designed to assess individuals' interests, strengths, and preferences to guide career decision-making, providing information on suitable occupational matches based on their responses.

37. System of Interactive Guidance and Information (SIGI): SIGI is a computer-based career guidance system that offers interactive tools and resources to help individuals explore career options, make informed decisions, and plan their educational and occupational paths.

38. Dislocated worker: A dislocated worker refers to an individual who has lost their job due to various circumstances, such as layoffs, business closures, or technological changes, and may require assistance and resources for reemployment and career transition.

39. If a counselor advises a female to stay clear of police work because it is a "male occupation," he is discriminating on the basis of a gender bias.

40. The primary purpose of an aptitude test is to serve as a predictor for future performances.

Questions and Answers

This section covers twenty questions on the career development core area. Make sure to test your competency by going through each of them before moving to the next chapter.

1. Which of these is not a primary goal of career counseling?

    A. Increasing self-awareness and self-confidence
    B. Enhancing decision-making and problem-solving skills
    C. Assisting individuals in obtaining employment
    D. Providing financial planning advice

2. What is the first stage in Donald Super's career development theory?

    A. Exploration
    B. Growth
    C. Maintenance
    D. Establishment

3. According to Holland's RIASEC model, which type is characterized as practical, hands-on, and down-to-earth?

    A. Realistic
    B. Investigative
    C. Artistic
    D. Enterprising

4. Which career development theory proposes that career decisions are influenced by an individual's self-efficacy beliefs?

    A. Social Cognitive Career Theory
    B. Holland's Theory
    C. Super's Theory
    D. Krumboltz's Theory

5. Which term refers to the match between an individual's personality and their work environment?

    A. Person-job fit
    B. Person-organization fit
    C. Person-environment fit
    D. Person-career fit

6. In Super's career development theory, which stage is characterized by stabilizing one's work identity and making advancements?

    A. Exploration
    B. Growth
    C. Maintenance
    D. Establishment

7. Which career development theory emphasizes the importance of congruence between an individual's personality and their chosen career?

    A. Holland's Theory
    B. Krumboltz's Theory
    C. Social Cognitive Career Theory
    D. Super's Theory

8. Which assessment tool is commonly used to measure interests and match individuals with suitable careers?

    A. Myers-Briggs Type Indicator (MBTI)
    B. Strong Interest Inventory
    C. Minnesota Satisfaction Questionnaire (MSQ)
    D. Occupational Outlook Handbook (OOH)

9. According to the stages of career development proposed by Donald Super, which stage typically occurs during adolescence?

    A. Exploration
    B. Growth

C. Maintenance
D. Establishment

10. Which career development theory emphasizes the influence of social factors, such as family and cultural background, on career choices?

A. Krumboltz's Theory
B. Holland's Theory
C. Super's Theory
D. Social Cognitive Career Theory

11. Which factor refers to an individual's belief in their capability to successfully perform tasks and achieve career goals?

A. Self-efficacy
B. Locus of control
C. Self-concept
D. Self-esteem

12. Which type in Holland's RIASEC model is characterized as imaginative, intuitive, and creative?

A. Realistic
B. Investigative
C. Artistic
D. Enterprising

13. Who proposed the Theory of Work-Adjustment, which focuses on the match between individuals and their work environments?

A. John Holland
B. Frank Parsons
C. ohn Krumboltz
D. René Dawis and Lloyd Lofquist

14. Which career development theory suggests that career decisions are influenced by genetic endowments, environmental conditions, and learning experiences?

    A. Social Cognitive Career Theory
    B. Holland's Theory
    C. Super's Theory
    D. Krumboltz's Theory

15. Which approach to career counseling focuses on helping individuals explore and clarify their values, interests, and skills?

    A. Trait and factor approach
    B. Developmental approach
    C. Narrative approach
    D. Cognitive approach

16. According to Super's career development theory, which stage typically occurs during mid-adulthood?

    A. Exploration
    B. Growth
    C. Maintenance
    D. Establishment

17. Which career development theory proposes that individuals actively construct their careers through learning experiences, social interactions, and self-reflection?

    A. Holland's Theory
    B. Super's Theory
    C. Krumboltz's Theory
    D. Social Cognitive Career Theory

18. Which term refers to the internal factors that drive individuals to seek fulfillment and personal growth in their careers?

    A. Intrinsic motivation

B. Extrinsic motivation

C. Job satisfaction

D. Career aspirations

19. According to Holland's RIASEC model, which type is characterized as persuasive, sociable, and energetic?

A. Realistic

B. Investigative

C. Social

D. Enterprising

20. Which assessment tool is commonly used to assess an individual's personality traits and preferences in career decision-making?

A. Strong Interest Inventory

B. Myers-Briggs Type Indicator (MBTI)

C. Minnesota Satisfaction Questionnaire (MSQ)

D. Occupational Outlook Handbook (OOH)

In the next chapter, we will move on to counseling and helping relationships, which forms another of the core NCE areas.

Answer Key

Q.	1	2	3	4	5	6	7	8	9	10
A.	C	D	C	C	C	D	A	B	A	A

Q.	11	12	13	14	15	16	17	18	19	20
A.	A	C	D	D	B	C	D	A	D	B

Chapter Seven: Counseling and Helping Relationships

The stark reality of counseling relationships is that about fifty-seven percent of clients drop out of therapy after a single session (Schwartz, 2017). This means that to maintain strong counseling relationships, you have to focus on getting the client to choose good, and lasting change. In this chapter, we will go over the important terms that can help you form a better idea of this core NCE area. A lot of valuable information is available via study guides on Chegg.com, for those of you who have further interest in the topic.

Important Topics

- Building counselor and client relationships

  Building counselor and client relationships involve establishing rapport, trust, and empathy. Counselors employ active listening skills to demonstrate attentiveness and understanding. They use genuineness, demonstrating authenticity and congruence in their interactions. Cultural sensitivity ensures respect for diverse backgrounds. Ethical boundaries maintain professionalism and confidentiality. Collaborative goal-setting promotes shared decision-making.

- Person-centered approach

  In the person-centered approach, building counselor and client relationships involve creating a supportive and empathetic environment. Counselors exhibit unconditional positive regard, offering acceptance and non-judgmental attitudes towards clients. Active listening is crucial to understanding clients' experiences and feelings. Empathy allows counselors to understand and validate clients' perspectives. Genuineness promotes authenticity and unity in the therapeutic relationship.

- Additional counseling skills

In addition to building counselor and client relationships, additional counseling skills play a vital role in effective therapy. These skills include:

A. Reflective listening: Counselors use reflective listening to summarize and restate clients' thoughts and feelings, demonstrating understanding and validating their experiences.

B. Empathy: By empathizing with clients, counselors show deep understanding, compassion, and the ability to see things from their perspective.

C. Questioning and probing: Skillful questioning helps counselors gather relevant information, explore clients' concerns, and uncover underlying issues.

D. Psychoeducation: Providing clients with information about their concerns, treatment options, and coping strategies empowers them to participate in their healing process through informed decision-making.

E. Problem-solving: Counselors assist clients in identifying problems, exploring potential solutions, and developing practical strategies to address challenges.

F. Crisis intervention: When clients are in immediate distress or facing crises, counselors utilize crisis intervention techniques to provide support, stabilize the situation, and connect clients with appropriate resources.

G. Cognitive restructuring: This skill involves challenging negative or irrational thought patterns and helping clients develop healthier, more adaptive beliefs and perspectives.

H. Relaxation and stress management techniques: Counselors teach clients relaxation exercises, deep breathing, mindfulness, and other coping skills to manage stress, anxiety, and emotional regulation.

I.   Behavioral interventions: Counselors employ techniques such as goal setting, behavior modification, and reinforcement to help clients develop and reinforce positive behaviors.

J.   Cultural competence: Recognizing and respecting clients' cultural backgrounds and identities is essential for providing inclusive and effective counseling services.

- Initial phase of relationship building

During the initial phase of relationship building, counselors focus on establishing rapport and trust with clients. They create a safe and non-judgmental environment to foster open communication. Active listening and empathy are employed to demonstrate understanding and validate clients' experiences. The counselor conducts an initial assessment to gather relevant information about clients' presenting concerns, backgrounds, and goals. This assessment helps tailor the counseling approach to meet clients' specific needs. Building a collaborative and mutually respectful relationship sets the foundation for a therapeutic alliance where clients feel supported, heard, and empowered to embark on their journey of growth and change.

- Stages of positive interaction

In the exploration phase, counselors encourage clients to express and examine their emotions, thoughts, and concerns. This helps identify the core issues and establish a shared understanding. Consolidation involves integrating and synthesizing information, fostering insight and clarity. Collaborative planning follows, where the counselor and client work together to develop strategies, set goals, and determine steps toward change. Finally, the termination phase acknowledges progress, evaluates outcomes, and prepares clients for the transition out of counseling, ensuring a positive closure and continuation of growth beyond the therapeutic relationship.

- Transference

Positive and negative transference are two psychological phenomena that can occur in the therapeutic relationship. Positive transference is when a client projects positive feelings, such as admiration, onto the therapist, based on unconscious dynamics. This can foster trust, openness, and a sense of safety. On the other hand, negative transference involves the client projecting negative emotions or attitudes, such as anger or mistrust, onto the therapist. This may stem from past experiences or unresolved conflicts. Recognizing and addressing both positive and negative transference is important in therapy, as it allows for exploration, understanding, and the potential for healing and growth within the therapeutic relationship.

- Client resistance

Client resistance refers to how clients may demonstrate reluctance, hesitation, or opposition during the counseling process. Resistance often stems from underlying fears, discomfort, or protective mechanisms. It can manifest as avoidance of certain topics, defensiveness, minimization of issues, or challenges to the counselor's suggestions or interventions.

- Phases of a crisis period

Gerald Caplan's model of crisis intervention identifies several phases within a crisis period. It begins with an initial threat or event that triggers a response, where individuals utilize their coping skills to manage the situation. However, if the crisis escalates, the initial attempts at coping may prove unsuccessful, leading to increased distress. This leads to the acute stress phase, where anxiety intensifies, and the fight or flight response may be engaged. As the crisis climaxes, all previous solutions have failed, resulting in severe personality disorganization. This may manifest as severe depression, violent behavior, or suicidal thoughts. Recognizing these phases helps counselors provide appropriate support and interventions to address clients' needs during times of crisis.

- 7 stages of crisis intervention

Crisis intervention involves a series of stages to effectively support individuals in crisis. It begins with conducting thorough biopsychosocial assessments to understand the individual's unique circumstances. The counselor then makes prompt contact and works to establish rapport, creating a safe and trusting environment. The crisis's specific problems and underlying causes are identified through collaborative exploration. Counseling is provided to understand the emotional context and provide support. Coping strategies and alternative solutions are developed, leading to the implementation of an action plan for treatment. Follow-up and ongoing evaluations are conducted to monitor progress and adjust interventions as needed. These stages ensure a comprehensive and responsive approach to crisis intervention, helping individuals navigate through challenging times.

- The integrative ACT intervention model

The integrative ACT (Acceptance and Commitment Therapy) intervention model combines several key components to promote psychological flexibility and well-being. It emphasizes acceptance of present experiences, mindfulness, and clarifying personal values. The model incorporates cognitive defusion, committed action, and self-as-context to help individuals develop a flexible relationship with their thoughts and emotions. The integrative ACT intervention model aims to enhance psychological resilience and promote meaningful, value-driven lives by fostering acceptance, values-based action, and mindfulness.

- Critical Incident Stress Debriefing

Critical Incident Stress Debriefing (CISD) is an intervention tool to address the psychological impact of critical incidents on individuals who have experienced or witnessed traumatic events. CISD typically takes place within 24-72 hours after the incident. It involves an open discussion where participants can share their experiences and feelings in a safe and confidential environment. The CISD team provides support, psychoeducation, and coping strategies to help individuals overcome stress and manage the effects of secondary trauma. The goal of CISD is to promote psychological well-being, resilience, and recovery in the aftermath of critical incidents.

- Rational problem-solving process

  Rational problem-solving process involves a systematic approach to addressing problems. It includes identifying and defining the problem, generating possible solutions, evaluating options, implementing the best solution, and reflecting on the outcome to make necessary adjustments.

- Intuitive problem-solving

  Intuitive problem-solving relies on instinct, gut feelings, and past experiences to make quick decisions. It involves trusting one's intuition and relying on patterns, hunches, or subconscious cues to arrive at a solution without following a formal step-by-step process. It can be effective for making rapid decisions when time is limited or when there is a lack of available information.

- Extinguishing

  Extinguishing in counseling is a therapeutic technique used to diminish or eliminate unwanted behaviors by removing the reinforcement that maintains them. Through collaborative identification of the target behavior, assessment of antecedents and consequences, and analysis of the behavior's function, the counselor helps the client develop strategies to weaken the behavior and replace it with more adaptive alternatives. This process involves removing or reducing the reinforcing consequences associated with the behavior to promote positive change.

- Allen Ivy's three types of empathy

  Allen Ivey proposed three types of empathy in counseling: basic empathy, additive empathy, and subtractive empathy. Basic empathy involves understanding the client's thoughts and feelings without necessarily sharing them. Additive empathy goes a step further by actively connecting with the client's experiences, emotions, and perspective. Subtractive empathy involves temporarily setting aside one's own experiences to fully immerse oneself in the client's world. These three types of empathy help counselors develop a deep understanding of clients' experiences, fostering a strong therapeutic alliance and facilitating effective interventions.

- Warning signs to consider before expressing personal feelings

  Before expressing personal feelings, it is important to be aware of certain warning signs. These include a power imbalance in the relationship, potential harm to the therapeutic alliance, a lack of client readiness or receptiveness, a deviation from the client's goals, or the potential for personal disclosure to overshadow the client's needs. Additionally, suppose personal feelings arise from unresolved personal issues or biases. If so, it is crucial to seek supervision or consultation to ensure that the client's best interests remain the focus of the therapeutic process.

- Support system

  A support system in counseling refers to the network of individuals who provide emotional, practical, and social support to the client. This system typically includes friends, family members, or other trusted individuals who offer encouragement, understanding, and guidance during challenging times. The support system plays a vital role in the client's healing and growth by providing a safe space for expressing emotions, offering different perspectives, and assisting with problem-solving. The counselor helps the client identify and strengthen existing support systems or helps the client develop new ones to enhance their overall well-being.

- Maslow's hierarchy of needs

  Maslow's hierarchy of needs proposes a hierarchical model of human needs. It suggests that individuals have a set of fundamental needs that must be fulfilled in a specific order to achieve self-actualization. The hierarchy consists of five levels: physiological needs (such as food and shelter), safety needs (including personal security and stability), belongingness and love needs (such as social relationships), esteem needs (including self-esteem and recognition), and self-actualization needs (fulfilling one's full potential). As each lower level is satisfied, individuals strive to fulfill needs at higher levels to reach their highest level of personal growth.

- Structured and unstructured helping relationships

  Structured helping relationships in counseling involves clear goals, established boundaries, and a formalized approach, such as cognitive-behavioral therapy. Unstructured helping relationships, on the other hand, are more open-ended and flexible, allowing clients to explore their thoughts and feelings freely, often seen in person-centered therapy.

- External stress, internal distress, and transitional stress

  Internal distress refers to the emotional and psychological responses that arise within an individual due to external stressors, manifesting as anxiety, depression, or other negative emotions. External stress refers to environmental or situational factors that place pressure or demands on an individual, such as work deadlines or financial difficulties. Transitional stress is the stress experienced during significant life transitions, such as ending a relationship or moving somewhere new, which can disrupt a person's sense of stability and require adjustment to new circumstances.

Questions and Answers

There are twenty MCQs to test your preparedness for counseling and helping relationships core area of the NCE. Ensure to complete this test before moving to the next chapter.

1. What is the primary objective of counseling?

    A. Problem-solving
    B. Emotional venting
    C. Personal growth and positive change
    D. Providing advice

2. Which counseling approach emphasizes the importance of empathy and unconditional positive regard?

    A. Psychodynamic therapy
    B. Cognitive-behavioral therapy
    C. Solution-focused therapy
    D. Person-centered therapy

3. What is an essential component of active listening in counseling?

    A. Offering advice
    B. Sharing personal experiences
    C. Demonstrating empathy and understanding
    D. Interrupting the client

4. Which counseling theory focuses on identifying and changing irrational thoughts and beliefs?

    A. Psychodynamic theory
    B. Gestalt therapy
    C. Cognitive-behavioral therapy
    D. Existential therapy

5. Which is an example of a directive counseling technique?

    A. Reflective listening
    B. Paraphrasing
    C. Giving advice
    D. Active listening

6. What describes the emotional bond and trust between a counselor and client?

    A. Transference
    B. Countertransference
    C. Rapport
    D. Resistance

7. Which ethical principle emphasizes the counselor's obligation to maintain confidentiality?

    A. Autonomy
    B. Non-maleficence
    C. Beneficence
    D. Fidelity

8. What is the primary purpose of using open-ended questions in counseling?

    A. To gather specific information
    B. To direct the conversation
    C. To encourage exploration and self-reflection
    D. To challenge the client's beliefs

9. Which counseling approach focuses on identifying and building upon a client's strengths and resources?

    A. Narrative therapy
    B. Solution-focused therapy
    C. Psychoanalytic therapy
    D. Adlerian therapy

10. What is the term for a therapist's ability to make sense of and share the feelings of a client?

    A. Transference
    B. Empathy
    C. Countertransference
    D. Sympathy

11. Which stage of the counseling process involves exploring the client's concerns and identifying their goals?

    A. Assessment
    B. Intervention
    C. Termination
    D. Planning

12. Which counseling approach emphasizes the importance of unconscious processes and childhood experiences?

    A. Person-centered therapy
    B. Psychodynamic therapy
    C. Rational emotive behavior therapy
    D. Gestalt therapy

13. Which ethical principle requires counselors to provide accurate and honest information to clients?

    A. Fidelity
    B. Autonomy
    C. Non-maleficence
    D. Veracity

14. What is the term for a counselor's response that captures the essence of the client's message?

    A. Paraphrasing
    B. Reflecting

    C. Summarizing

    D. Clarifying

15. Which counseling approach focuses on exploring the meaning and purpose of life?

    A. Existential therapy

    B. Family systems therapy

    C. Dialectical behavior therapy

    D. Rational emotive behavior therapy

16. What describes the counselor's ability to remain nonjudgmental and accepting of the client?

    A. Transference

    B. Congruence

    C. Unconditional positive regard

    D. Resistance

17. Which stage of the counseling process involves implementing interventions and strategies to address the client's concerns?

    A. Assessment

    B. Planning

    C. Termination

    D. Intervention

18. Which counseling approach explores the client's unconscious conflicts and defense mechanisms?

    A. Cognitive-behavioral therapy

    B. Humanistic therapy

    C. Psychodynamic therapy

    D. Gestalt therapy

19. What describes a counselor's ability to be genuine, authentic, and transparent with the client?

   A. Transference
   B. Empathy
   C. Congruence
   D. Resistance

20. Which ethical principle requires counselors to do no harm and prioritize the client's well-being?

   A. Autonomy
   B. Non-maleficence
   C. Beneficence
   D. Justice

In the next chapter, we will discuss group counseling and group work.

Answer Key

Q.	1	2	3	4	5	6	7	8	9	10
A.	C	D	C	C	C	C	D	C	B	B

Q.	11	12	13	14	15	16	17	18	19	20
A.	A	B	D	B	A	C	D	C	C	B

Chapter Eight: Group Counseling and Group Work

Group counseling and group work are essential components of the NCE exam. Understanding the unique challenges and opportunities presented in group counseling and the ability to create a supportive and inclusive environment is crucial for counselors to effectively work with diverse populations and facilitate positive group experiences. Topics covered may include group dynamics, stages of group development, leadership styles, ethical considerations, facilitation skills, and interventions specific to group settings (*NCE STUDY NOTES - Group Therapy | PDF | Group Psychotherapy | Psychotherapy*, n.d.).

In this chapter, we will cover some of the most important keywords and terms related to this core NCE area. You can find more such information on quizlet.com.

Important points

1. Before the 1960s, most counseling happened in a dyadic relationship, involving an interaction between two individuals.
2. A group has a defined membership, unity and interaction, and a common purpose.

3. Raymon Corsini, a psychotherapy author, called the 1940s the modern era for group work. During this time, two organizations came up for group therapy. These were the American Society for Group Psychotherapy and Psychodrama (assicuated with Jacob Moreno, 1942) and the American Group Psychotherapy Association (associated with Samuel Richard Slavson, 1943).

4. Alfred Adler and Jesse B. Davis contributed to developing group work and prefaced group movement.

5. Primary groups serve as a preventive measure, aiming to proactively mitigate and prevent potential problems from arising.

6. Groups are secondary and have disturbances and difficulties.

7. Tertiary groups deal with more severe pathology in comparison to secondary groups.

8. Group norms govern group roles and acceptable behaviors.

9. During WWII, the shortage of individual therapists made group therapy flourish in the United States.

10. Group content is how discussions and transactions happen.

11. Group cohesiveness indicates forces that bind group members as a whole.

12. Experts agree that group therapy is of longer duration.

13. One advantage of group work is that a counselor can see more clients in a given period. One disadvantage is that a counselor can become preoccupied with group processes and leave individual issues unexamined.

14. The risk shift phenomenon believes group decisions are less conservative than the average group member's decision before the group discussion.

15. T in T-groups stands for training.

16. Most assertive training groups are behavioristic and highly structured.

17. Weight Watchers is a support or self-help group.

18. Private screening can be superior in terms of counselor-client interaction.

19. An essential trait for group members is trust.

20. A closed group promotes cohesiveness.

21. A disadvantage of an open group is a member who begins after the first meeting has missed information or experiences.

22. When a group member speaks, the counselor should try to face the group member.

23. A group setting has a seating arrangement where clients can sit where they wish. In this setting, an Asian American leader and an Asian American client would likely sit close by.

24. Groups encourage the concept of universality.
25. In the late 1930s, researchers identified three basic leadership styles: autocratic, democratic, and laissez-faire. The autocratic leader controls a group, and the laissez-faire leader prefers little involvement.
26. The democratic style is most preferable. Sam Gladdig called this a facilitator style.
27. Coleadership is desirable because the group can go on even if one leader is absent. Two leaders can focus on group dynamics better than one leader since two individuals will have better observational skills, and leaders can process their feelings between sessions.
28. Coleadership counters burnout and promotes safety.
29. Gerald Corey, a writer on group therapy, believes participation in a therapeutic and in a leader's group is necessary for an effective group leader.
30. Most experts agree that an effective adult counseling group has five or six to eight members.
31. Most experts agree that two hours is plenty of time, even when critical issues are being examined.
32. An ethical leader will discuss group risks during the initial session with a client.
33. An adept group leader will attempt to safeguard clients against risks and work to reduce them.
34. During the initial group session, the leader explained no smoking and cursing would be permitted. This is known as setting ground rules.
35. Group norms refer to acceptable behaviors in a group.
36. A dynamic group is always changing.
37. A common group weakness is a lack of goal-setting.
38. A group member who insists on asking other members inappropriate questions is known as an interrogator.
39. A nonassertive follower will go with what everyone else decides.
40. A gatekeeper may covertly wish they were running the group.

Questions and Answers

Now, we will cover 20 questions relevant to this core area. Remember to practice all of them before moving to the next chapter.

1. Which term refers to the interactions and relationships among group members?

    A. Group norms
    B. Group dynamics
    C. Group cohesion
    D. Group process

2. The stage of group development characterized by conflict and power struggles is:

    A. Forming
    B. Storming
    C. Norming
    D. Performing

3. Group counseling techniques are used to:

    A. Establish group norms
    B. Facilitate change within a group
    C. Resolve conflicts among group members
    D. Develop individual counseling skills

4. The ethical principle of maintaining the privacy of group members' personal information is known as:

    A. Confidentiality
    B. Autonomy
    C. Non-maleficence
    D. Veracity

5. The recognition and appreciation of individual differences within a group is known as:

    A. Group cohesion
    B. Group empowerment
    C. Group diversity
    D. Group inclusion

6. Which is NOT a stage of group development?

    A. Adjourning
    B. Transforming
    C. Norming
    D. Performing

7. Group feedback is important because it:

    A. Establishes group norms
    B. Encourages conflict resolution
    C. Facilitates self-awareness and personal growth
    D. Enhances group cohesion

8. The process of reaching consensus or making choices within a group is known as:

    A. Group decision-making
    B. Group empowerment
    C. Group conflict resolution
    D. Group feedback

9. Who is known for developing the "forming, storming, norming, performing" model of group development?

    A. Carl Rogers
    B. Bruce W. Tuckman
    C. Kurt Lewin
    D. Elizabeth L. Holloway

10. Which term refers to the number of members in a group?

    A. Group dynamics
    B. Group size
    C. Group roles
    D. Group norms

11. Group counseling is particularly effective in schools because it:

    A. Addresses individual counseling needs
    B. Provides social support and skill development
    C. Enhances teacher-student relationships
    D. Focuses on parent involvement

12. Conflict resolution strategies in group counseling aim to:

    A. Avoid conflicts altogether
    B. Ignore conflicts and focus on individual growth
    C. Address and resolve conflicts constructively
    D. Promote power struggles among group members

13. Which theorist is known for their work on existential group therapy?

    A. Irvin D. Yalom
    B. Carl Rogers
    C. Kurt Lewin
    D. Elizabeth T. Rankin

14. Group empowerment focuses on:

    A. Establishing group norms and expectations
    B. Enhancing the power and autonomy of group members
    C. Resolving conflicts among group members
    D. Promoting individual counseling skills

15. The founder of psychodrama and sociometry is:

    A. Irvin D. Yalom
    B. Carl Rogers
    C. J. L. Moreno
    D. Samuel T. Gladding

16. The Cooperative Learning model, emphasizing collaborative group work, was developed by:

    A. David W. Johnson and Roger T. Johnson
    B. Irvin D. Yalom and Molyn Leszcz
    C. Carolyn Sherif and Elizabeth T. Rankin
    D. Samuel T. Gladding and J. L. Moreno

17. Feminist group therapy focuses on:

    A. Addressing gender-specific issues in group counseling
    B. Enhancing group cohesion and leadership skills
    C. Promoting cultural diversity within the group
    D. Resolving conflicts among group members

18. Conflict resolution strategies developed by Peter T. Coleman focus on:

    A. Enhancing group cohesion
    B. Managing conflicts within groups, organizations, and communities
    C. Resolving conflicts through force and aggression
    D. Ignoring conflicts to maintain group harmony

19. The understanding and management of group dynamics is emphasized in which approach to group work?

    A. Systems-Centered approach by Yvonne M. Agazarian
    B. Task-centered approach by Paul H. Ephross
    C. Cooperative Learning approach by David W. Johnson and Roger T. Johnson
    D. Existential approach by Irvin D. Yalom

20. In a healthy group, members:

    A. Assume a role and never change it
    B. Have no roles
    C. Are flexible and can change roles
    D. Spend a great deal of time practicing role reversal

In the next chapter, we will move on to the core area of assessment and testing.

Answer Key

Q.	1	2	3	4	5	6	7	8	9	10
A.	B	B	B	A	C	B	C	A	B	B

Q.	11	12	13	14	15	16	17	18	19	20
A.	B	C	A	B	C	A	A	B	A	C

Chapter Nine: Assessment and Testing

In counseling, being prepared to assess and test clients is one of the most important components of the profession. This core area focuses on the skills and knowledge you need to effectively measure, assess, and evaluate your clients. It covers topics related to methods, ethical considerations, psychometrics, and interpreting assessment results. This section will cover some important key terms and points that will help you do well in the exam. Many more such points are covered in quizlet.com.

Important Points

1. Appraisal: Professionally administered assessment tools and tests used to evaluate, measure, and gain insight into clients' abilities and characteristics.
2. Behavioral Observation: An assessment method used to document and record the behavior of clients or research subjects for analysis and evaluation.
3. Bell Curve: A graphical representation of data distribution that resembles the shape of a bell, indicating a normal distribution pattern.
4. Correlation Coefficient: A statistical measure describing the relationship between two variables and indicating how they influence each other. Positive correlation means both variables move in the same direction, while negative correlation indicates opposite directions.

5. Dichotomous Items: Test items that offer two opposing choices: yes/no or true/false options.
6. Difficulty Index: A measure that indicates the proportion of examinees who answer test items correctly, reflecting the test's difficulty level.
7. External Validity: The extent to which a study's results can be generalized or applied to a bigger population beyond the study sample.
8. Forced Choice Items: Survey items that require respondents to choose from two or more specific response options, leaving no room for open-ended answers.
9. Free Choice Test: Also known as Liberal Choice, it allows respondents to provide subjective or open-ended responses rather than selecting from predetermined options.
10. Halo Effect: The tendency to form a generalized positive impression based on limited information or specific characteristics.
11. Horizontal Test: A test that covers material from various subjects or domains, providing a comprehensive assessment.
12. Ipsative Format: A testing approach that measures an individual's preferences in responding to problems, people, and procedures, without comparing the results to others.
13. Likert Scale: A rating scale used to measure attitudes or opinions by asking respondents to indicate their agreement or disagreement via a statement series.
14. Mean: The average value arrived at by adding all given test scores and dividing the resulting sum by the number of scores.
15. Median: The middle or central value in an ordered list of scores or data. An even data set typically determines the median by averaging the two middle numbers.
16. Measure: A score assigned to assess traits, behaviors, or actions within an individual.
17. Mode: The most frequently occurring score or value in a group of test scores. If multiple scores occur equally, the test does not have a mode.
18. Normative Format: A testing approach that compares individuals' performance or characteristics to a larger normative group.
19. Objective Test Items: Standardized questions with clear correct or incorrect answers, leaving no room for interpretation.
20. Obtrusive Measurement: Assessment tools, such as observations, are conducted with the knowledge and awareness of the individual being assessed.

21. Percentile: A ranking scale ranging from 1 to 100 that indicates the percentage of individuals who scored at or below a particular level.

22. Projective Test: A type of assessment that presents individuals with ambiguous stimuli to elicit responses that reveal their unconscious desires, thoughts, or beliefs.

23. Psychological Assessment: An informal process of testing, interviews, or observations used to determine the psychological needs, strengths, and challenges of an individual, often leading to more formal testing if necessary.

24. Psychological Test: A specific measurement or assessment conducted to evaluate, diagnose, or develop treatment plans. It can include personality assessments, intelligence tests, projective tests, or diagnostic batteries.

25. Psychometrics: The study or process of psychological measurement, including the development, validation, and interpretation of assessment tools.

26. Q-Sort: A self-assessment procedure where individuals sort items relative to one another along a dimension, such as agree/disagree or importance.

27. Range: The difference between the top and lowest scores in a group of test scores, indicating the spread or variability.

28. Rapport: The establishment of trust, understanding, respect, and liking between two individuals is crucial for building an effective therapeutic relationship.

29. Rating Scale: A process of measuring degrees of experience, attitudes, or opinions through questions that allow respondents to rate or evaluate.

30. Regression to the Mean: The statistical tendency of a data series to move closer to the average or center of a distribution over time.

31. Stanine (STAndard NINE): A nine-point scaled score used to convert a test score into a single digit, ranging from zero to nine.

32. T-Score: A specific scoring method used in psychometrics to standardize test scores and convert them into positive numbers. T-Scores represent the number of standard deviations a score is from the mean, which is typically set at 50.

33. Test: A measuring device or procedure designed to assess individuals' knowledge, abilities, skills, or other characteristics.

34. Test Battery: A group or set of tests administered to the same group of individuals, often scored against a standardized criterion, to obtain a comprehensive assessment of various aspects or domains.

35. Trait: A method of describing individuals based on observable

characteristics that are unique and distinguishable, representing enduring patterns of behavior, thoughts, or emotions.

36. Variance: A measure of how individuals in a group or data set vary from the mean, indicating the spread or dispersion of scores.

37. Vertical Test: Refers to administering tests on the same subject to different levels or age groups, allowing for comparisons across different developmental stages or educational levels.

38. Z-Score: Also known as a standard score, it measures the number of standard deviations a raw score is from the mean. A Z-Score of zero represents the mean, with positive values indicating scores above the mean and negative values below the mean.

39. Aptitude Test: Assess the capacity for learning and can be used in job applications. Examples include the Differential Aptitude Test (DAT), Wonderlic Cognitive Ability Test, and Career Ability Placement Survey (CAPS). They measure abstract/conceptual, verbal, and/or numerical reasoning.

40. Intelligence Test: Measure mental capacity and potential. Examples include WISC, WAIS, WPPSI, Woodcock-Johnson, and Kaufman Assessment Battery for Children.

41. Occupational Test: Evaluate skills, values, or interests related to vocational and occupational choices. Examples include the O*NET Interest Profiler, Career Assessment Inventory, and Self-Directed Search.

42. Personality Test: Provide insight into personality traits, underlying beliefs, and behaviors. They can be objective (rating scale-based) or projective (self-reporting-based). Examples include the Myers-Briggs Type Inventory (MBTI), Minnesota Multiphasic Personality Inventory (MMPI-2), Beck Depression Inventory, and Rorschach (inkblot) test.

43. Ethical Issues in Testing: Counselors must have proper training and certifications, administer appropriate tests, obtain informed consent from clients, maintain the confidentiality of test results, and ensure tests are validated and unbiased.

44. Francis Galton: Studied intelligence in the late 1800s, coined the term "Eugenics," and believed intelligence was genetically determined and could be enhanced through selective parenting.

45. J.P. Guilford: Conducted psychometric studies on intelligence and creativity in the early 1900s and critiqued one-dimensional intelligence tests for not capturing human diversity in abilities, thinking, and creativity.

46. Charles Spearman: Introduced statistical analysis to intelligence testing and proposed the G Factor Theory for general intelligence, which influenced the analysis of intelligence tests.

47. Binet and Simon: Developed the first test to identify children who would succeed in school, introduced the concept of mental age, and their work formed the basis for modern intelligence testing.

48. Raymond Cattell and John Horn: Developed theories of fluid and crystallized intelligence in the 1940s, distinguishing between the ability to solve novel problems and accumulating skills and knowledge over time.

Questions and Answers

This section covers 20 questions and answers on the core area of assessment and testing. Please finish them before moving to the next chapter.

1. What is the process of establishing uniform procedures for administering and scoring a test to ensure consistency and comparability of results called?

   A. Standardization
   B. Reliability
   C. Validity
   D. Normalization

2. Which statistical measure describes the relationship between two variables and indicates how they influence each other?

   A. Mean
   B. Mode
   C. Median
   D. Correlation coefficient

3. Who developed the first test to identify children who would succeed in school and introduced the concept of mental age?

   A. Francis Galton
   B. J.P. Guilford
   C. Charles Spearman
   D. Binet and Simon

4. What is the percentage of individuals in the normative group who scored at or below a particular score called?

   A. Raw score
   B. Standard score
   C. Percentile rank
   D. Criterion score

5. What is the term used to describe systematic errors or distortions in test results that are unfair or discriminatory toward certain groups?

    A. Reliability
    B. Bias
    C. Validity
    D. Norming

6. Which type of assessment involves ongoing evaluation during the learning process to provide feedback and guide instruction?

    A. Formative assessment
    B. Summative assessment
    C. Authentic assessment
    D. Diagnostic assessment

7. Who proposed the theory of multiple intelligences, suggesting that individuals possess different types of intelligence?

    A. Howard Gardner
    B. Raymond Cattell
    C. John Horn
    D. Charles Spearman

8. What is the transformed score that provides information about an individual's performance relative to the average performance of a normative group called?

    A. Raw score
    B. Standard score
    C. Z-score
    D. T-score

9. Who is known for the concept of emotional intelligence?

    A. Sigmund Freud
    B. Carl Jung
    C. Daniel Goleman
    D. Erik Erikson

10. What is the term used for the degree to which a test measures consistently and produces stable results over time?

    A. Validity
    B. Reliability
    C. Standardization
    D. Norming

11. Who developed the theory of multiple-choice tests and introduced the concept of item difficulty and discrimination?

    A. Francis Galton
    B. J.P. Guilford
    C. Charles Spearman
    D. Frederic Lord

12. What is the process of interpreting test scores and making meaningful inferences about an individual's abilities, traits, or characteristics called?

    A. Standardization
    B. Norming
    C. Scoring
    D. Test interpretation

13. Which type of validity focuses on whether a test accurately predicts or correlates with a criterion measure?

    A. Content validity
    B. Concurrent validity
    C. Construct validity
    D. Face validity

14. Who developed the theory of intelligence consisting of general intelligence and specific abilities?

    A. Raymond Cattell
    B. John Horn

C. Charles Spearman
D. Howard Gardner

15. What is used to describe the extent to which a test covers an intended content or domain?

    A. Content validity
    B. Criterion validity
    C. Construct validity
    D. Face validity

16. Who introduced the concept of the bell curve and the normal distribution pattern?

    A. Francis Galton
    B. J.P. Guilford
    C. Charles Spearman
    D. Carl Gauss

17. Which kind of validity denotes the extent to which a test will measure what it is intended to?

    A. Content validity
    B. Concurrent validity
    C. Construct validity
    D. Face validity

18. Who developed the theory of cognitive development and the stages of intellectual development concepts?

    A. Sigmund Freud
    B. Jean Piaget
    C. Erik Erikson
    D. Lawrence Kohlberg

19. What is used to describe the process of selecting items from a larger item pool to create a test or assessment?

    A. Standardization
    B. Sampling
    C. Scoring
    D. Item analysis

20. Who is considered the father of modern intelligence testing and developed the first intelligence test?

    A. Alfred Binet
    B. Carl Jung
    C. John Dewey
    D. Sigmund Freud

In the next chapter, we discuss the final core area, which is Research and Program Evaluation.

Answer Key

Q.	1	2	3	4	5	6	7	8	9	10
A.	A	D	D	C	B	A	A	B	C	B

Q.	11	12	13	14	15	16	17	18	19	20
A.	D	D	B	C	A	D	D	B	B	A

Chapter Ten: Research and Program Evaluation

To be the best at your job, you have to be on a constant quest for improvement. You must refine your approaches and skills and evaluate the programs you study and use on clients. In this section, we cover some terms that could help you answer any questions that come in the NCE.

Important Points

1. R. A. Fisher pioneered hypothesis testing. A hypothesis represents an educated guess or a hunch that can be tested via the experimental model.
2. Type I and Type II errors are known as alpha and beta errors. The former happens when a researcher rejects a null hypothesis when this is actually true. The second happens when they accept a null when it is false.
3. Behaviorists often employ N=1. This is known as intensive experimental design. The first step here is to take a baseline measure, which could be "N" or the number of persons being subjected to a study. This becomes the case study of an approach.
4. The empirical or 68-95-99.7 rule believes that in normal distribution, 68% of scores come under plus/minus 1 standard deviation of the mean; 95% fall with two SDs, and 99.7% fall within three SDs. Almost all scores fall between three SDs of the mean.
5. In a frequency polygon or basic curve, the point of maximum concentration is called Mode.

6. The median represents a middle score when data gets arranged from the highest to lowest values.

7. If a group of first-semester students take the NCE, the scores distribution will be positively skewed.

8. The x-axis is a horizontal line drawn under a frequency distribution.

9. The interval scale has numbers that are scaled at equal distances with no absolute zero point. Most tests used in school systems belong to this group. You can add and subtract with them but not multiply or divide.

10. The simplest form of descriptive research is a survey.

11. A researcher sees a client group isn't receiving counseling but improving. Her hypothesis is that the attention she has given to them is curative. This represents the Hawthorne effect.

12. A researcher can run a true experiment with systematic sampling.

13. An operational definition outlines a procedure.

14. A researcher studies a single session of counseling in which a counselor treats a client's phobia using a paradoxical strategy. Then, they write in their research report that paradox is the treatment of choice for phobics. This is an example of inductive since the research goes from specific to generalization.

15. Reliability refers to stability and consistency of research instruments and measures.

16. Quantitative research methods look at applying tools like experiments, surveys, and statistical analysis.

17. Qualitative research methods include observations, interviews, and content analysis.

18. Data analysis includes descriptive and inferential statistics and qualitative data analysis.

19. Program evaluation is understanding the process of evaluating programs to determine their impact and effectiveness.

20. Needs assessment identifies specific needs of target populations for program development.

21. Outcome evaluation determines if programs achieve intended goals and objectives.

22. Formative evaluation comprises ongoing evaluations during program development and implementation to guide modifications and improvements.

23. Logic models are visual representations of program theory, activities, inputs, outputs, and outcomes.

Questions and Answers

Before moving on to the practice tests, spend some time finishing the 20 MCQs in this core area.

1. What is the goal of needs assessment in program evaluation?

    A. To determine program outcomes
    B. To identify target populations
    C. To assess program implementation
    D. To evaluate program effectiveness

2. Which of the following research designs involves manipulating an independent variable and randomly assigning participants?

    A. Correlational design
    B. Descriptive design
    C. Experimental design
    D. Quasi-experimental design

3. Which is a measure of the consistency and stability of research measures or instruments?

    A. Reliability
    B. Validity
    C. Generalizability
    D. Accuracy

4. In program evaluation, outcome evaluation focuses on:

    A. Program implementation
    B. Stakeholder involvement
    C. Program effectiveness
    D. Ethical considerations

5. Which is an example of a qualitative research method?

    A. Survey
    B. Experiment
    C. Content analysis
    D. Statistical analysis

6. Which type of sampling technique involves selecting participants based on specific characteristics to ensure representativeness?

    A. Convenience sampling
    B. Purposive sampling
    C. Random sampling
    D. Stratified sampling

7. What is the process of evaluating programs and interventions to determine their effectiveness and impact?

    A. Needs assessment
    B. Process evaluation
    C. Program evaluation
    D. Outcome evaluation

8. Which refers to the accuracy and appropriateness of research measures in measuring what they intend to measure?

    A. Reliability
    B. Validity
    C. Generalizability
    D. Precision

9. Which type of evaluation focuses on ongoing assessments during program development and implementation?

    A. Formative evaluation
    B. Summative evaluation
    C. Process evaluation

    D. Impact evaluation

10. Which statistical analysis technique is used to examine relationships between variables and determine the strength and direction of the relationship?

    A. T-test
    B. Analysis of variance (ANOVA)
    C. Correlation analysis
    D. Chi-square test

11. What is the term for engaging key stakeholders in the evaluation process to ensure their input and perspectives are considered?

    A. Utilization-focused evaluation
    B. Participatory evaluation
    C. Collaborative evaluation
    D. Stakeholder evaluation

12. Which type of evaluation focuses on the implementation and delivery of programs?

    A. Outcome evaluation
    B. Summative evaluation
    C. Process evaluation
    D. Impact evaluation

13. Which is an example of a quantitative research method?

    A. Case study
    B. Focus group
    C. Content analysis
    D. Survey

14. What is the visual representation of program theory, inputs, activities, outputs, and outcomes called?

    A. Logic model

    B. Conceptual framework
    C. Research design
    D. Program matrix

15. Which of the following ethical principles emphasizes the importance of protecting participants' privacy and confidentiality?

    A. Informed consent
    B. Beneficence
    C. Justice
    D. Confidentiality

16. Which of the following data analysis techniques involves organizing, summarizing, and presenting data meaningfully?

    A. Descriptive statistics
    B. Inferential statistics
    C. Qualitative data analysis
    D. Content analysis

17. What type of research design is often used when one cannot manipulate an independent variable?

    A. Experimental design
    B. Correlational design
    C. Quasi-experimental design
    D. Descriptive design

18. What is the process of using research findings to inform decision-making and program improvement called?

    A. Utilization-focused evaluation
    B. Participatory evaluation
    C. Collaborative evaluation
    D. Stakeholder evaluation

19. What type of evaluation assesses the overall effectiveness and impact of a program?

    A. Formative evaluation
    B. Summative evaluation
    C. Process evaluation
    D. Impact evaluation

20. Which refers to the accuracy and precision of research measures?

    A. Reliability
    B. Validity
    C. Generalizability
    D. Representativeness

In the next chapter, we move on to two full-lengh exams to help you get even better at preparing for the NCE exam.

Answer Key

Q.	1	2	3	4	5	6	7	8	9	10
A.	B	C	A	C	C	D	C	B	A	C

Q.	11	12	13	14	15	16	17	18	19	20
A.	B	C	D	A	D	A	C	A	B	A

Chapter Eleven:
Full-Length Exam

This section covers a mock exam done in the style of the NCE. You will get questions based on all core areas. The answers are at the end of the set. Attempt to answer all of them before going to confirm them, and best of luck!

1.   Which of these describes a dual relationship?

A. A counselor who counsels their neighbor.
B. A counselor working as a bartender part-time.
C. A counselor hiring a former client as an intern.
D. A counselor who's friends with a client's sibling.

2.   Which represents a requirement to get informed consent?

A. The counselor must give a detailed diagnosis to their client.
B. They must explain potential risks and benefits of treatment.
C. They must disclose all client information to a third party.
D. They must get written consent from client's family members.

3.   Which describes a boundary violation?

A. A counselor shares their personal problems with a client.
B. A counselor refers a client to a specialist for additional treatment
C. A counselor charges a higher fee to more complicated clients.
D. A counselor attends a client's graduation ceremony as a show of support.

4.   Which is true regarding the use of touch in counseling?

   A. Touch should be avoided.
   B. Touch can be used if the client consents.
   C. Touch should only be used if the client initiates it.
   D. Touch is only appropriate for certain cultural groups.

5.   Which is NOT a potential ethical issue related to technology-assisted counseling?

   A. Informed consent
   B. Data privacy
   C. Appropriate use of social media
   D. Proper use of secure technology platforms

6.   Which is NOT a recommended approach for addressing cultural differences in counseling?

   A. Encouraging the client to assimilate into the dominant culture
   B. Learning about the client's cultural background
   C. Recognizing and addressing one's own biases
   D. Adapting counseling techniques to fit the client's cultural background

7.   Which is an example of a boundary crossing in counseling?

   A. Giving the client a ride home after a session
   B. Accepting a small gift from the client during the holidays
   C. Dating a former client after a reasonable amount of time has passed
   D. All of the above

8.   Which is an example of a boundary violation in counseling?

   A. Offering advice outside the scope of one's training and expertise
   B. Maintaining appropriate physical distance from the client during sessions
   C. Refusing to provide services to a client based on personal beliefs or biases

D. Using derogatory language or engaging in discriminatory behavior toward a client

9. Which is not an element of ethical decision-making in counseling?

   A. Recognizing the ethical dilemma
   B. Identifying possible courses of action
   C. Consulting with colleagues or supervisors
   D. Choosing the most profitable course of action.

10. Among the following, which is NOT a recommended way to address potential ethical violations by a colleague?

   A. Directly confronting the colleague about the violation
   B. Reporting the violation to a supervisor or licensing board
   C. Ignoring the violation and continuing to work with the colleague
   D. Seeking consultation from an ethics expert

11. Which of the following situations would need a counselor to break confidentiality and warn a potential victim?

   A. A client reports feeling depressed
   B. A client discloses a plan to harm a specific individual
   C. A client discusses past drug use
   D. A client expresses anger toward a family member

12. The duty to warn clause:

   A. Requires counselors to report any criminal activity disclosed by a client
   B. Allows counselors to disclose confidential information to protect a client from harm
   C. Mandates that counselors report any suicidal ideation expressed by a client
   D. Requires counselors to disclose confidential information to prevent harm to a specific, identifiable person.

13. The American Counseling Association (ACA) Code of Ethics:

   A. Provides guidelines for ethical and legal issues related to the practice of counseling
   B. Regulates the licensure of counselors in all states
   C. Establishes reimbursement rates for counseling services
   D. Mandates that all counseling sessions be recorded and made available to clients upon request

14. The purpose of state licensure laws for professional counselors is to:

   A. Ensure that counselors have the necessary training and qualifications to provide services to clients
   B. Regulate reimbursement rates for counseling services
   C. Establish ethical standards for the counseling profession
   D. Limit the number of counselors in a given geographic area

15. Informed consent in the counseling relationship refers to:

   A. A counselor's obligation to maintain confidentiality with clients
   B. A client's agreement to participate in counseling and their understanding of the nature of counseling
   C. A counselor's ability to diagnose and treat mental health disorders
   D. A client's agreement to pay for counseling services

16. Which is NOT a requirement of the privacy rule by HIPAA (Health Insurance Portability and Accountability Act) for counselors?

   A. Counselors must obtain written consent before sharing clients' protected health information (PHI)
   B. Counselors must provide clients with a notice of privacy practices
   C. Counselors must obtain a client's signature on a release of information form before sharing PHI
   D. Counselors must keep clients' PHI confidential and secure

17. When conducting research with clients, counselors must:

    A. Obtain informed consent and ensure confidentiality
    B. Only involve clients diagnosed with a specific mental health disorder
    C. Share research findings with clients' insurance companies
    D. Offer financial compensation to clients for their participation

18. When a counselor receives a subpoena requesting a client's records, the counselor should:

    A. Immediately comply with the subpoena and release the records
    B. Consult with an attorney to determine the course of action
    C. Notify the client and seek their permission to release the records
    D. Ignore the subpoena and continue to maintain confidentiality

19. The principle of nonmaleficence in counseling refers to:

    A. Counselors' obligation to provide clients with accurate and truthful information.
    B. Counselors' commitment to avoiding harm and preventing potential harm to clients
    C. The ethical requirement to keep professional boundaries and avoid dual relationships.
    D. The responsibility to promote social justice and advocate for clients' rights

20. In the counseling process, the initial stage that involves gathering information about the client's concerns, background, and history is called:

    A. Treatment planning
    B. Intake
    C. Assessment
    D. Diagnosis

21. Which is an open-ended question in an intake interview?

    A. "Have you ever received a mental health diagnosis before?"

B. "Are you currently taking any medications?"

C. "What brings you to counseling today?"

D. "How often do you experience anxiety?"

22. A counselor is using a standardized test to assess a client's intelligence. This type of assessment is an example of:

A. Projective assessment

B. Diagnostic assessment

C. Objective assessment

D. Behavioral assessment

23. The primary purpose of conducting a mental health assessment is to:

A. Identify the client's specific diagnosis

B. Determine the severity of the client's symptoms

C. Assess the client's strengths and challenges

D. Provide a recommendation for treatment

24. When administering an assessment, it is important for counselors to consider the client's cultural background because:

A. Culture can influence the client's understanding and response to assessment items

B. Cultural background is irrelevant to the assessment process

C. Assessments are universally applicable and unbiased across cultures

D. Cultural background has no impact on the client's mental health

25. Which of the following assessment methods involves observing and documenting the client's behavior in natural settings?

A. Interviews

B. Self-report measures

C. Case formulation

D. Behavioral assessment

26. The process of assigning labels to clients' presenting problems based on a recognized classification system is known as:

    A. Diagnosis
    B. Treatment planning
    C. Case conceptualization
    D. Assessment

27. Which is true regarding the DSM-5 (Diagnostic and Statistical Manual)?

    A. It provides guidelines for conducting therapy sessions with clients.
    B. It is a comprehensive assessment tool used to evaluate cognitive functioning.
    C. It is a prevalent classification system for diagnosing mental disorders.
    D. It focuses primarily on physical health conditions and diseases.

28. In the context of assessment, reliability refers to:

    A. The extent to which this assessment can measure what it claims to measure
    B. The consistency and stability of assessment results over time
    C. The ability of an assessment to differentiate between different groups of individuals
    D. The extent to which an assessment produces similar results when administered by different clinicians

29. Which is an example of a structured interview?

    A. A counselor asking open-ended questions to explore the client's thoughts and feelings
    B. A counselor using a set of predetermined questions to gather specific information from the client
    C. A counselor using nonverbal cues to convey empathy and understanding
    D. A counselor engaging in reflective listening to validate the client's experiences

30. When conducting a risk assessment, counselors should prioritize:

    A. Identifying the client's immediate goals for counseling
    B. Gathering detailed information about the client's childhood experiences
    C. Assessing the client's potential for harm to self or others
    D. Developing a treatment plan based on the client's diagnosis

31. A counselor using a Likert scale to measure the intensity of a client's symptoms is utilizing:

    A. Projective assessment
    B. Objective assessment
    C. Diagnostic assessment
    D. Behavioral assessment

32. In the context of assessment, validity refers to:

    A. The degree to which this assessment can measure what it claims to
    B. The consistency and stability of assessment results over time
    C. The ability of an assessment to differentiate between different groups of individuals
    D. The extent to which an assessment produces similar results when administered by different clinicians

33. The main purpose of a clinical formulation or case conceptualization is to:

    A. Determine the appropriate dosage and frequency of medication for the client
    B. Identify the underlying causes and contributing factors to the client's difficulties
    C. Assign a diagnosis to the client based on their symptoms
    D. Establish specific goals for treatment

34. When conducting an assessment for suicide risk, it is important for counselors to:

    A. Avoid asking direct questions about suicide to prevent distressing the client
    B. Focus solely on the client's current functioning and not inquire about past suicidal ideation
    C. Use open-ended questions to explore the client's reasons for living
    D. Ask direct and specific questions about the client's suicidal thoughts and intentions

35. Which of the following assessment methods involves using pictures, drawings, or projective techniques to assess the client's unconscious conflicts and motivations?

    A. Interviews
    B. Self-report measures
    C. Case formulation
    D. Projective assessment

36. The process of making predictions about the client's future behavior, based on the information gathered during assessment, is known as:

    A. Diagnosis
    B. Treatment planning
    C. Case conceptualization
    D. Prognosis

37. When conducting a comprehensive assessment, counselors should gather information about the client's:

    A. Immediate family members' mental health history
    B. Childhood experiences and family background
    C. Political and religious beliefs
    D. Personal preferences for treatment modalities

38. The purpose of providing feedback to clients after the assessment process is to:

    A. Establish rapport and build a therapeutic alliance
    B. Persuade clients to agree with the counselor's diagnostic impressions
    C. Educate clients about the limitations of the assessment results
    D. Collaboratively develop treatment goals and interventions

39. Which is NOT considered a clinical focus area in counseling?

    A. Substance abuse
    B. Depression
    C. Career development
    D. Marketing strategies

40. The therapeutic approach that emphasizes the importance of the client's current thoughts and beliefs is:

    A. Cognitive-behavioral therapy (CBT)
    B. Solution-focused brief therapy (SFBT)
    C. Psychoanalysis
    D. Person-centered therapy

41. Which of the following is a clinical focus area that involves helping individuals cope with major life transitions?

    A. Anxiety disorders
    B. Personality disorders
    C. Grief and loss
    D. Eating disorders

42. A counselor specializing in working with couples and helping them improve their communication skills is likely to focus on:

    A. Trauma counseling
    B. Marriage and family therapy
    C. Career counseling

D. Crisis intervention

43. The clinical focus area that involves working with individuals who have experienced traumatic events is:

A. Addiction counseling
B. Trauma counseling
C. Child and adolescent counseling
D. Geriatric counseling

44. A counselor working with children and adolescents to address behavioral issues and emotional difficulties is likely to specialize in:

A. Family counseling
B. Play therapy
C. Career counseling
D. Addiction counseling

45. The clinical focus area that involves helping individuals with career exploration, decision-making, and job-related challenges is:

A. Career counseling
B. Group counseling
C. Crisis intervention
D. Couples counseling

46. A counselor working with individuals struggling with substance abuse and addiction is likely to use:

A. Cognitive-behavioral therapy (CBT)
B. Psychoanalysis
C. Gestalt therapy
D. Solution-focused brief therapy (SFBT)

47.   The clinical focus area that involves working with patients impacted by mood disorders, such as depression and bipolar disorder, is:

A. Mood disorders counseling
B. Psychodynamic therapy
C. Existential therapy
D. Psychopharmacology

48.   A counselor who works with individuals struggling with body image issues and disordered eating patterns is likely to specialize in:

A. Substance abuse counseling
B. Career counseling
C. Eating disorders counseling
D. Trauma counseling

49.   The clinical focus area that involves helping individuals improve their interpersonal relationships and develop effective communication skills is:

A. Couples counseling
B. Career counseling
C. Group counseling
D. Child and adolescent counseling

50.   A counselor working with individuals who have experienced sexual trauma is likely to use:

A. Play therapy
B. Trauma-focused cognitive-behavioral therapy (TF-CBT)
C. Psychodynamic therapy
D. Rational emotive behavior therapy (REBT)

51.   The clinical focus area that involves working with individuals who have personality disorders and helping them manage their symptoms is:

A. Personality disorders counseling
B. Existential therapy

C. Solution-focused brief therapy (SFBT)
D. Geriatric counseling

52. A counselor who works with older adults to address issues related to aging, loss, and life transitions is likely to specialize in:

   A. Geriatric counseling
   B. Career counseling
   C. Child and adolescent counseling
   D. Addiction counseling

53. The clinical focus area that involves working with individuals who have anxiety disorders, such as generalized anxiety disorder and panic disorder, is:

   A. Anxiety disorders counseling
   B. Psychodynamic therapy
   C. Gestalt therapy
   D. Family counseling

54. A counselor working with individuals who have experienced domestic violence and helping them heal from the trauma is likely to use:

   A. Solution-focused brief therapy (SFBT)
   B. Trauma-focused cognitive-behavioral therapy (TF-CBT)
   C. Rational emotive behavior therapy (REBT)
   D. Psychopharmacology

55. The clinical focus area that involves working with families to address relational conflicts and improve communication is:

   A. Family counseling
   B. Career counseling
   C. Couples counseling
   D. Group counseling

56. A counselor who works with individuals struggling with self-esteem and self-worth issues is likely to specialize in:

    A. Existential therapy
    B. Psychodynamic therapy
    C. Humanistic therapy
    D. Play therapy

57. The male prototype of Freud's Electra complex is:

    A. Superego
    B. Ego
    C. Id
    D. Oedipus

58. During vocational evaluation of a client who has disabilities, the counselor is at the workplace assessment stage. The stage that follows is:

    A. Rehabilitation evaluation
    B. Physical conditioning
    C. Risk assessment
    D. Functional capacity evaluation

59. The clinical focus area that involves working with eating disorder-impacted individuals, such as anorexia nervosa and bulimia nervosa, is:

    A. Eating disorders counseling
    B. Psychodynamic therapy
    C. Existential therapy
    D. Child and adolescent counseling

60. A counselor who works with individuals struggling with addictions and helps them develop strategies for recovery is likely to specialize in:

    A. Psychodynamic therapy
    B. Addiction counseling
    C. Geriatric counseling

D. Solution-focused brief therapy (SFBT)

61.   Which of these theories considers conflict resolution and the cessation of destructive behaviors to be crucial therapeutic goals?

A. Couples therapy
B. Existential therapy
C. Psychodynamic method
D. Family counseling

62.   HIPAA involves all of these except?

A. Sharing information regulation
B. Interstate Variabilities
C. Regulation of insurance policies
D. Protects client privacy

63.   The clinical focus area that involves working with individuals who have sexual and gender identity issues is:

A. Sexuality counseling
B. Psychodynamic therapy
C. Existential therapy
D. Psychopharmacology

64.   Which of these does not represent a regression?

A. A means of defense
B. A psychoanalytic idea
C. Rational emotive therapy
D. Freudian notion

65.   The clinical focus area that involves working with individuals who have psychotic disorders, such as schizophrenia, is:

A. Psychotic disorders counseling
B. Family counseling

C. Group counseling

D. Psychopharmacology

66. A counselor working with individuals who have experienced military trauma and helps them reintegrate into civilian life is likely to use:

A. Military counseling

B. Trauma-focused cognitive-behavioral therapy (TF-CBT)

C. Rational emotive behavior therapy (REBT)

D. Play therapy

67. The clinical focus area that involves working with individuals who have developmental disabilities is:

A. Developmental disabilities counseling

B. Career counseling

C. Psychopharmacology

D. Couples counseling

68. A counselor who works with individuals struggling with anger management issues and helps them develop healthy coping strategies is likely to specialize in:

A. Solution-focused brief therapy (SFBT)

B. Psychodynamic therapy

C. Existential therapy

D. Anger management counseling

69. The clinical focus area that involves working with individuals who have obsessive-compulsive disorder (OCD) and helping them manage their symptoms is:

A. OCD counseling

B. Psychodynamic therapy

C. Gestalt therapy

D. Family counseling

70. A group of women with ages evaluated for IQ levels is subjected to a research on the same day. The study is?

    A. Stratified sample study
    B. Cross-sectional study
    C. Longitudinal study
    D. Systemic sample study

71. The clinical focus area that involves working with individuals who have autism spectrum disorder is:

    A. Autism spectrum disorder counseling
    B. Child and adolescent counseling
    C. Psychopharmacology
    D. Couples counseling

72. A counselor who works with individuals struggling with stress management and helps them develop relaxation techniques is likely to specialize in:

    A. Solution-focused brief therapy (SFBT)
    B. Psychodynamic therapy
    C. Existential therapy
    D. Stress management counseling

73. During a session with a client who displays antisocial conduct, the client makes suggestive gestures to the counselor. What should be the counselor's appropriate reaction?

    A. Stop touching me and leave
    B. Why did you do this? What do you want to prove?
    C. Keep your hands on your lap; it's not required to touch the counselor.
    D. I will report you

74. A counselor's attitude toward leisurely activities should be?

    A. It's restful and taken during work

B. Vacation time
C. Not acknowledged to clients
D. Avocations

75. The clinical focus area that involves working with individuals with phobias and helping them overcome their fears is:

A. Phobia counseling
B. Career counseling
C. Couples counseling
D. Psychopharmacology

76. A counselor who works with individuals struggling with self-harm behaviors and helps them develop healthier coping mechanisms is likely to specialize in:

A. Solution-focused brief therapy (SFBT)
B. Psychodynamic therapy
C. Existential therapy
D. Self-harm counseling

77. The clinical focus area that involves working with individuals who have gambling addiction is:

A. Gambling addiction counseling
B. Psychodynamic therapy
C. Gestalt therapy
D. Family counseling

78. A counselor working with individuals who have experienced natural disasters and helps them rebuild their lives is likely to use:

A. Trauma counseling
B. Group counseling
C. Rational emotive behavior therapy (REBT)
D. Career counseling

79. The clinical focus area that involves working with individuals who have bipolar disorder and helping them manage their mood swings is:

   A. Bipolar disorder counseling
   B. Psychodynamic therapy
   C. Existential therapy
   D. Couples counseling

80. A counselor who works with individuals struggling with body dysmorphia and helps them develop a positive body image is likely to specialize in:

   A. Body dysmorphia counseling
   B. Child and adolescent counseling
   C. Psychopharmacology
   D. Geriatric counseling

81. Which is correct when it comes to assessing clients with disabilities?

   A. Standardized and customized test settings yield equivalent results.
   B. Disability has no effect on test outcomes.
   C. Test modifications are widely accepted.
   D. More research is needed to determine whether standardized and customized test circumstances provide equivalent results.

82. Norms are important for which of the following?

   A. Parallel comparative forms
   B. Test reliability
   C. Behavior sample meanings
   D. Normal distribution of scores

83. A fervently devout client believes her infirmity is punishment for her evil conduct. Which of these Interventions will aid her most?

   A. Self-help materials
   B. Referral to a self-help group
   C. Pastoral counseling
   D. Psychotherapy

84.   Which behavior should be considered while creating an eating disorder care plan?

    A. Weight goals
    B. Self-harming behaviors
    C. Sexual issues
    D. Motivation to change

85.   Appraisal comprises all of these barring?

    A. Individual tests
    B. Observing
    C. Group tests
    D. Clinical intervention

86.   Which is a key component of treatment planning?

    A. Assessing client strengths and resources
    B. Prescribing medication
    C. Setting rigid treatment goals
    D. Ignoring client preferences

87.   Which of the following interventions is ineffective in developing a bulimia patient's eating habits?

    A. Address responses to various food types
    B. Maintaining a food journal
    C. Daily assessment of ratings of compliance with dietary restrictions
    D. The client has to dine in the dining area.

88.   Which is NOT a common step in the treatment planning process?

    A. Identifying treatment goals
    B. Assessing client readiness for change
    C. Administering psychological tests
    D. Developing an action plan

89.   What is the client's role in the treatment planning process?

A. To follow the counselor's instructions without question
B. To provide informed consent for treatment
C. To dictate the entire treatment approach
D. To passively receive treatment without input

90.   Which is an example of a measurable treatment goal?

A. Enhancing self-esteem
B. Increasing insight
C. Improving family dynamics
D. Decreasing symptoms of anxiety by 50%

91.   What is the purpose of creating short-term objectives in treatment planning?

A. To evaluate client progress
B. To satisfy insurance requirements
C. To establish long-term treatment goals
D. To set unrealistic expectations for clients

92.   Which is a characteristic of a well-written treatment plan?

A. It is solely focused on the counselor's agenda
B. It includes vague and ambiguous language
C. It is based on evidence-based practices
D. It lacks client involvement and collaboration

93.   When should treatment goals and objectives be reviewed and revised?

A. Only at the beginning of treatment
B. Quarterly during the treatment process
C. When the counselor feels like making changes
D. Whenever client needs or circumstances change

94. What is the significance of cultural factors in treatment planning?

    A. Cultural factors have no impact on treatment outcomes
    B. Cultural factors should be ignored in treatment planning
    C. Treatment plans should be culturally sensitive and responsive
    D. Cultural factors are relevant only for certain populations

95. Which is an example of an appropriate treatment intervention?

    A. Imposing personal values on the client
    B. Using unproven and unsupported techniques
    C. Adapting interventions to meet client needs
    D. Discouraging client participation in therapy

96. How does the theoretical orientation of the counselor influence treatment planning?

    A. It limits the counselor's ability to be flexible in treatment
    B. It ensures that all clients receive the same interventions
    C. It provides a framework for understanding client issues
    D. It prohibits the use of evidence-based practices

97. What is the purpose of monitoring client progress during treatment?

    A. To prove the effectiveness of the counselor's interventions
    B. To compare the client to others in similar situations
    C. To assess the need for medication adjustments
    D. To make informed decisions about treatment modifications

98. Which is a potential challenge in treatment planning?

    A. Lack of ethical guidelines
    B. Overemphasis on client preferences
    C. Inadequate counselor training
    D. Excessive reliance on standardized assessments

99. What is the importance of involving clients in treatment planning?

A. It increases counselor authority and control
B. It ensures compliance with legal requirements
C. It promotes client ownership and investment in the process
D. It allows counselors to avoid responsibility for treatment outcomes

100. Which is an example of a nonverbal communication technique in counseling?

A. Active listening
B. Paraphrasing
C. Eye contact
D. Reflection

101. What is the primary goal of empathic responding in counseling?

A. To provide advice and solutions
B. To show understanding and convey acceptance
C. To challenge the client's beliefs
D. To redirect the conversation

102. Which counseling technique involves restating the client's message in your own words?

A. Paraphrasing
B. Reflecting feelings
C. Summarizing
D. Questioning

103. What is the purpose of using open-ended questions in counseling?

A. To gather specific information
B. To validate the client's emotions
C. To encourage exploration and reflection
D. To provide guidance and direction

104. Which counseling skill involves maintaining focused attention on the client?

    A. Paraphrasing
    B. Reflecting feelings
    C. Active listening
    D. Summarizing

105. What is the primary purpose of using reflection of feelings in counseling?

    A. To challenge the client's beliefs
    B. To clarify the client's thoughts
    C. To validate and explore the client's emotions
    D. To redirect the conversation

106. Which counseling technique involves condensing and organizing the client's words into a brief statement?

    A. Paraphrasing
    B. Reflecting feelings
    C. Summarizing
    D. Questioning

107. A client with severe agoraphobia shows up for a session but feels breathless as soon as the counselor shuts the door. The counselor should respond by:

    A. Telling the client to breathe
    B. Asking if the client will feel better with the door open
    C. Touching the client's hand to soothe them
    D. Convincing the client the door must be closed to ensure privacy and they are safe with the counselor

108. Which is an example of a closed-ended question?

    A. "Tell me more about that."
    B. "What are your thoughts on the matter?"
    C. "Do you feel sad?"
    D. "How does that make you feel?"

109. Which counseling technique involves exploring the client's reasons for change?

    A. Paraphrasing
    B. Reflecting feelings
    C. Summarizing
    D. Motivational interviewing

110. A disaster management counselor is mentally and physically exhausted, and they lack compassion for the client's problems. What exactly is the counselor's issue?

    A. Burnout
    B. Compassion fatigue
    C. Depression
    D. PTSD

111. Which of the following is a micro skill used in counseling to demonstrate empathy?

    A. Open-ended questions
    B. Reflective istening
    C. Challenging assumptions
    D. Providing advice

112. Which counseling technique involves asking the client for clarification or more information?

    A. Paraphrasing
    B. Reflecting feelings
    C. Summarizing
    D. Questioning

113. What is the purpose of using silence in counseling?

    A. To create discomfort and challenge the client
    B. To allow for reflection and deeper processing

C. To redirect the conversation

D. To gather specific information

114. Which counseling skill involves using body language and verbal cues to show attentiveness?

    A. Paraphrasing
    B. Reflecting feelings
    C. Active listening
    D. Summarizing

115. What is the primary goal of confrontation in counseling?

    A. To challenge the client's beliefs
    B. To provide advice and solutions
    C. To redirect the conversation
    D. To show understanding and convey acceptance

116. Which counseling technique involves reflecting the emotional content of the client's message?

    A. Paraphrasing
    B. Reflecting feelings
    C. Summarizing
    D. Questioning

117. What is the main purpose of using scaling questions in counseling?

    A. To explore the client's values and beliefs
    B. To challenge the client's assumptions
    C. To assess the client's motivation and progress
    D. To provide guidance and direction

118. Which counseling skill involves observing and interpreting non-verbal cues?

    A. Paraphrasing

B. Reflecting feelings
C. Active listening
D. Summarizing

119. What is the primary purpose of psychoeducation in counseling?

    A. To challenge the client's beliefs
    B. To provide information and enhance understanding
    C. To redirect the conversation
    D. To show empathy and acceptance

120. Carl Rogers proposed that giving unconditional love and support to another person is an example of which of the following?

    A. Unconditional positive regard
    B. Existentialist concept
    C. Self-actualization
    D. Worth

121. What is the prime purpose of using self-disclosure in counseling?

    A. To challenge the client's beliefs
    B. To provide advice and solutions
    C. To show empathy and establish rapport
    D. To redirect the conversation

122. Which is an example of an advanced empathy skill?

    A. Reflective listening
    B. Active listening
    C. Summarizing
    D. Reflecting content and feelings

123. What is the primary goal of cognitive restructuring in counseling?

    A. To challenge the client's beliefs
    B. To provide advice and solutions
    C. To redirect the conversation

D. To explore the client's emotions

124. The archway model of self-concept determinant was designed by?

    A. John Holland
    B. John Krumboltz
    C. Linda Gottfredson
    D. Donald Super

125. A counselor notes that one of the individuals in a support group regularly dominates the conversations and bothers others. What can be said about it?

    A. Group blocking
    B. Group theme
    C. Group pattern
    D. Group direction

126. Which counseling technique involves using metaphorical stories or examples to convey a message?

    A. Paraphrasing
    B. Reflecting feelings
    C. Summarizing
    D. Using analogies

127. What is the primary goal of solution-focused brief therapy?

    A. To explore the client's past experiences
    B. To challenge the client's beliefs
    C. To redirect the conversation
    D. To identify and work towards solutions

128. James-Lange theory of arousal and emotion includes which of these?

    A. Physiological reaction comes before emotions.
    B. Emotional responses occur prior to physiological reactions.

C. Emotional and physical responses co-occur.

D. Emotional and physical responses are not related.

129. A depressed client engages in self-harming activity and has persistent feelings of inferiority and failure. The counselor feels that changing this client's thoughts can end or change his depression. What exactly is the purpose of this therapy?

    A. Rational emotive therapy (RET)
    B. Averse conditioning
    C. Operant conditioning
    D. Psychoanalysis

130. Which counseling technique involves exploring the client's resistance to change?

    A. Paraphrasing
    B. Reflecting feelings
    C. Summarizing
    D. Working through resistance

131. What is the primary goal of behavioral activation in counseling?

    A. To challenge the client's beliefs
    B. To provide advice and solutions
    C. To redirect the conversation
    D. To increase engagement in positive behaviors

132. Which counseling skill involves guiding the client towards exploring alternatives and considering different perspectives?

    A. Paraphrasing
    B. Reflecting feelings
    C. Active listening
    D. Summarizing

133. What is the main purpose of using normalization in counseling?

    A. To challenge the client's beliefs
    B. To provide advice and solutions
    C. To redirect the conversation
    D. To reassure the client that their experiences are common

134. Which counseling technique involves exploring the client's strengths and resources?

    A. Paraphrasing
    B. Reflecting feelings
    C. Summarizing
    D. Resource identification

135. What is the primary goal of psychoanalytic therapy?

    A. To challenge the client's beliefs
    B. To provide advice and solutions
    C. To redirect the conversation
    D. To explore unconscious processes and unresolved conflicts

136. Which counseling skill involves providing a brief statement that captures the essence of the client's message?

    A. Paraphrasing
    B. Reflecting feelings
    C. Summarizing
    D. Questioning

137. What is the purpose of grounding techniques in counseling?

    A. To challenge the client's beliefs
    B. To provide advice and solutions
    C. To redirect the conversation
    D. To promote present-moment awareness and reduce anxiety

138. Which counseling technique involves exploring the client's options and potential courses of action?

    A. Paraphrasing
    B. Reflecting feelings
    C. Summarizing
    D. Problem-solving

139. What is the primary goal of person-centered therapy?

    A. To challenge the client's beliefs
    B. To provide advice and solutions
    C. To redirect the conversation
    D. To create a supportive and accepting therapeutic environment

140. "Collective Unconscious" and "archetypes" are two terms coined by

    A. Emile Durkheim
    B. Carl Jung
    C. Sigmund Freud
    D. Aaron Beck

141. What is the main purpose of using reframing in counseling?

    A. To challenge the client's beliefs
    B. To provide advice and solutions
    C. To redirect the conversation
    D. To offer alternative perspectives and interpretations

142. Which counseling technique involves exploring the client's fears and concerns related to change?

    A. Paraphrasing
    B. Reflecting feelings
    C. Summarizing
    D. Addressing ambivalence

143. What is the primary goal of behavioral therapy?

    A. To challenge the client's beliefs
    B. To provide advice and solutions
    C. To redirect the conversation
    D. To modify maladaptive behaviors

144. Which counseling skill involves providing a brief overview of what is covered in the session?

    A. Paraphrasing
    B. Reflecting feelings
    C. Summarizing
    D. Questioning

145. What is the purpose of relaxation techniques in counseling?

    A. To challenge the client's beliefs
    B. To provide advice and solutions
    C. To redirect the conversation
    D. To reduce stress and promote self-regulation

146. Which counseling technique involves exploring the client's self-talk and identifying negative or distorted thinking patterns?

    A. Paraphrasing
    B. Reflecting feelings
    C. Summarizing
    D. Cognitive restructuring

147. What is the primary purpose of motivational interviewing?

    A. To explore the client's past experiences
    B. To challenge the client's beliefs
    C. To redirect the conversation
    D. To enhance motivation for change

148. Which is a core attribute of effective counselors?

    A. Authority
    B. Judgmental attitude
    C. Empathy
    D. Superiority

149. Which core attribute involves being honest and trustworthy with clients?

    A. Respect
    B. Congruence
    C. Empathy
    D. Authenticity

150. Which core attribute involves maintaining a positive regard for clients, regardless of their actions or behaviors?

    A. Respect
    B. Congruence
    C. Empathy
    D. Unconditional positive regard

151. Which core attribute involves being genuine and authentic in the counseling relationship?

    A. Respect
    B. Congruence
    C. Empathy
    D. Boundaries

152. Gilbert Wrenn's The Counselor in a Changing World (1962) emphasized which role as paramount in the counseling profession?

    A. Neurotic needs
    B. Collective group needs
    C. Developmental needs
    D. Individual needs

153. Which of these signifies the bond of confidence and mutual understanding between a counselor and their client?

    A. Therapeutic alliance
    B. Window of opportunity
    C. Therapeutic window
    D. Clubhouse model

154. Which core attribute involves being non-judgmental and accepting of the client's thoughts, feelings, and behaviors?

    A. Respect
    B. Congruence
    C. Empathy
    D. Open-mindedness

155. Which core attribute involves being aware of and managing one's own biases and prejudices?

    A. Respect
    B. Congruence
    C. Empathy
    D. Cultural competence

156. Which core attribute involves treating clients with dignity and honoring their autonomy?

    A. Respect
    B. Congruence
    C. Empathy
    D. Assertiveness

157. Which of these is an important part of Albert Bandura's cognitive behavioral therapy approaches?

    A. Catharsis
    B. Aversive conditioning

C. Token economy

D. Self-efficacy

158. Hypnosis is best described as?

    A. Mind game
    B. Coercion
    C. Deep relaxation state
    D. Drug-induced mental state

159. Which of these enables a researcher to locate cause and effect?

    A. Naturalistic observation
    B. Experiment
    C. Survey
    D. Correlation

160. Which core attribute involves respecting and protecting the client's privacy and confidentiality?

    A. Respect
    B. Congruence
    C. Empathy
    D. Boundaries

Answer Key

Q.	1	2	3	4	5	6	7	8	9	10	11	12	13	14	15	16
A.	C	B	A	B	D	A	B	D	D	C	B	D	A	A	B	C

Q.	17	18	19	20	21	22	23	24	25	26	27	28	29	30	31	32
A.	A	B	B	B	C	C	C	A	D	A	C	B	B	C	B	A

Q.	33	34	35	36	37	38	39	40	41	42	43	44	45	46	47	48
A.	B	D	D	D	B	D	D	A	C	B	B	B	A	A	A	C

Q.	49	50	51	52	53	54	55	56	57	58	59	60	61	62	63	64
A.	A	B	A	A	A	B	A	C	D	C	A	B	A	B	A	C

Q.	65	66	67	68	69	70	71	72	73	74	75	76	77	78	79	80
A.	A	A	A	D	A	B	A	D	C	D	A	D	A	A	A	A

Q.	81	82	83	84	85	86	87	88	89	90	91	92	93	94	95	96
A.	D	C	C	B	D	A	C	C	B	D	A	C	D	C	C	C

Q.	97	98	99	100	101	102	103	104	105	106	107	108	109	110	111	112
A.	D	C	C	C	B	A	C	C	C	C	B	C	D	B	B	D

Q.	113	114	115	116	117	118	119	120	121	122	123	124	125	126	127	128
A.	B	C	A	B	C	C	B	A	C	D	A	D	C	D	D	A

Q.	129	130	131	132	133	134	135	136	137	138	139	140	141	142	143	144
A.	A	D	D	D	D	D	D	A	D	D	D	B	D	D	D	C

Q.	145	146	147	148	149	150	151	152	153	154	155	156	157	158	159	160
A.	D	D	D	C	D	D	B	C	A	B	D	A	D	C	B	D

Answers And Explanations

1. (C) This is a dual relationship where the counselor has a professional and personal role that can pose ethical challenges.

2. (B) The counselor must explain all possible risks and benefits that could stem from treatment.

3. (A) A counselor sharing personal problems with a client engages in a boundary violation.

4. (B) Touch can be used as a therapeutic intervention tool, but only when there is explicit acknowledgment on behalf of the client.

5. (D) While ensuring the proper use of secure technology platforms is necessary for protecting a client's security and confidentiality, it is not an ethical issue per se.

6. (A) It is not appropriate for counselors to advise clients to assimilate into the dominant culture. Rather, the counselor should respect their individualities.

7. (B) This could cause a conflict of interest and should, therefore, be avoided.

8. (D) Counselors have to maintain respect when dealing with clients. They cannot use derogatory language or display discriminatory behavior.

9. (D) In counseling, the primary interest of the counselor should always be promoting the health and well-being of their client, not profit.

10. (C) It is not proper for the counselor to ignore violations and continue working with the client. Instead, they have to ensure that the situation is addressed and mitigated.

11. (B) In this case, the counselor has to warn the potential victim so that there is no harm caused.

12. (D) The duty to warn means counselors need to breach confidentiality and disclose information since there is foreseeable danger to an identifiable person.

13. (A) The ACA gives guidelines for ethical and legal issues surrounding the counseling practice.

14. (A) State licensure laws exist to protect the public by ensuring counselors have appropriate training and are professionally competent.

15. (B) Informed consent means the client is told about and voluntarily agrees to engage in the counseling process after learning all about the risks and benefits therein.

16. (C) HIPAA needs counselors to keep clients' protected health information secure and private, but getting a signature on a release of information form is not a specific requirement under the privacy rule.

17. (A) Clients need to be fully aware of the procedures, end goal, risks, and benefits of the research before they voluntarily agree to participate.

18. (B) Consulting with an attorney will help the counselor become aware of legal obligations and determine the appropriate response.

19. (B) This is an ethical principle emphasizing the counselor's responsibility to inflict no harm and ensure clients benefit from the process with minimal adverse effects.

20. (B) The intake stage is the initial one where the client gets relevant background information on the client, including their concerns, personal history, and background.

21. (C) An open-ended question leaves room for the client to reflect and give their answer. Option C allows the client to think about why they're in counseling without any limitations.

22. (C) Standardized tests like intelligence tests have pre-established rules and scoring policies, making them objective assessments.

23. (C) The primary purpose of this assessment is to get an understanding of the psychological, behavioral, and emotional patterns of the client and assess their challenges, symptoms, and strengths when it comes to treatment.

24. (A) Clients' cultural backgrounds impact how they approach life and, therefore, assessments should always be culturally sensitive.

25. (D) In behavioral assessment, the counselor observes and documents the client's behavior in natural settings to arrive at an understanding of their nature.

26. (A) Diagnosis is identifying and labeling the presenting problems of the client based on classification systems like the Diagnostic and Statistical Manual of Mental Disorders.

27. (C) The DSM-5 has been developed by the American Psychological Association to diagnose mental disorders.

28. (B) Reliability refers to the stability and consistency of assessment results and whether they will produce similar outcomes when administered multiple times.

29. (B) A structured interview involves a standard set of predetermined questions which the counselor uses to garner specific information from the client.

30. (C) When conducting a risk assessment, the primary concern for counselors is to understand the client's potential to cause self-harm or injury to others.

31. (B) Likert scales allow the rating of frequency and severity of symptoms on a scale, making it possible to have a structured and measurable objective assessment.

32. (A) Validity refers to the extent to which an assessment measures what it intends to and captures the concepts or constructs it claims to assess.

33. (B) The main purpose of clinical formulation and case conceptualization is to understand the client's issues in a holistic, comprehensive manner by integrating assessment information and getting a theoretical understanding of their problems.

34. (D) The counselor must ask about the client's thoughts, plans, intentions, and any previous attempts.

35. (D) This involves using drawings, pictures, and projective techniques to understand the client's motivations, conflicts, and underlying dynamics. Examples include the Thematic Apperception Test or TAT.

36. (D) Prognosis is making predictions about the client's future behavior and outcomes depending on gathered information during an assessment.

37. (B) Comprehensive assessments include knowledge about childhood experiences and family background of the clients.

38. (D) The goal of feedback is to help the client participate in and actively work to get involved in their own treatment.

39. (D) Clinical focus areas are specific domains wherein counselors specialize so they can address particular mental health issues. Marketing strategies are not related to this area.

40. (A) CBT emphasizes the significance of the client's current behaviors, beliefs, and thoughts and how they influence their psychological and emotional well-being.

41. (C) Grief and loss is a clinical focus area helping people cope with major life transitions like the loss of a loved one, divorce, or changes in personal circumstances.

42. (B) This clinical focus area addresses the challenges and dynamics within families and couples. A counselor working in this area tries to resolve conflicts, enhance communication and strengthen relationships between couples.

43. (B) This is a specialized area focused on helping people who have experienced traumatic life events.

44. (B) Play therapy allows children to express their feelings, thoughts, and experiences via play and other creative activities.

45. (A) Career counseling helps people with exploring, deciding, and navigating jobs and related challenges.

46. (A) CBT identifies maladaptive beliefs, thoughts, and behaviors related to substance use and helps people develop coping skills, and prevents relapse.

47. (A) This specifically focuses on those who have been impacted by mood disorders like bipolar and depression.

48. (C) A counselor specializing in eating disorders counseling can support people struggling with body image issues and disordered eating habits.

49. (A) Couples counseling helps individuals improve interpersonal relationships, enhance communication, build intimacy, and resolve conflicts.

50. (B) This is an evidence-based treatment approach that helps people, including children and adolescents, who have experienced trauma.

51. (A) Personality disorders counseling involves working with people who have personality disorders characterized by maladaptive behaviors, thoughts, and interpersonal troubles.

52. (A) Geriatric counseling helps clients cope with issues related to age and the related emotional troubles that may arise.

53. (A) This is a clinical focus area specifically addressing the treatment of anxiety disorders. Counselors working in this area help their patients manage anxiety symptoms, identify and counter anxious thoughts, build relaxation techniques and enhance coping skills.

54. (B) TF-CBT is an evidence-based approach that addresses the impact of trauma and focuses on helping people process such experiences.

55. (A) This focuses on working with families to address communication issues, relational conflicts, and rebuild or strengthen relationships.

56. (C) Also known as person-centered therapy, this is used in case someone is struggling with self-esteem and worth issues. This emphasizes on a person's inherent ability to self-heal and self-determine.

57. (D) During the phallic stage of Freud's psychosexual development, a child enters a stage of conflict involving the same-sex parent, which manifests as Oedipus in the case of male children.

58. (C) After a vocation and a workplace, risk assessments are made.

59. (A) Eating disorders counseling focuses on working with people who struggle with eating disorders like bulimia nervosa, anorexia nervosa, and binge-eating disorder.

60. (B) Addiction counselors give guidance, support, and interventions to help clients overcome their addictions, develop recovery strategies and maintain sobriety.

61. (A) Couples therapy is focused on resolving conflicts and damaging practices.

62. (B) HIPAA is a national law and does not look at interstate variabilities.

63. (A) Sexuality counseling is a subset of counseling that focuses on assisting individuals in navigating and dealing with challenges linked to their sexual orientation and gender identity.

64. (C) Sigmund Freud stipulated regression as a coping strategy for those dealing with extremely traumatic situations in their lives. They might go back to their obsessive stage of psychosexual development. When faced with extreme stress, an individual with oral fixation may suck their thumb.

65. (A) Psychotic disorders counseling treats schizophrenia, schizoaffective disorder, and delusional disorder patients. This type of counselor supports, educates, and treats patients to improve their quality of life and rehabilitation.

66. (A) Military counseling helps veterans who have suffered trauma or other issues from their service.

67. (A) Developmental difficulties counseling helps those with autism spectrum disorder, intellectual disability, or Down syndrome. This area of counseling supports, advocates, and intervenes to help people with developmental disabilities enhance their daily lives, autonomy, and standard of life.

68. (D) Anger management therapy helps people with anger issues establish appropriate coping methods.

69. (A) OCD counseling helps people with repeated obsessions (intrusive and disturbing thoughts) and compulsions (repetitive behaviors or mental rituals).

70. (B) A cross-sectional study is an investigation of individuals who are comparable in every way except for the variable under consideration.

71. (A) Autism spectrum disorder (ASD) counseling emphasizes working with people who have been given the diagnosis of ASD, a neurodevelopmental illness marked by difficulties with social communication, repetitive habits, and limited interests.

72. (D) Stress management counseling focuses on assisting clients in developing effective stress management methods and coping abilities.

73. (C) Client boundaries must be maintained and respected by the counselor. Their reaction to unwanted behavior must be swift and firm without exhibiting anger or irritation.

74. (D) Avocations are discussed with clients by career counselors in order to increase client understanding.

75. (A) Phobia counseling helps people with specific phobias. To help people overcome phobias, counselors may use gradual exposure therapy, cognitive restructuring, and relaxation techniques.

76. (D) Self-harm therapy focuses on offering support to people who participate in self-harm behaviors such as cutting. Dialectical behavior therapy (DBT) and emotion-focused therapy (EFT) can assist clients learn better coping skills.

77. (A) This type of counselor helps clients understand their addiction, identify triggers, and develop methods to stop gambling.

78. (A) Trauma counseling helps people recover from stressful occurrences like natural disasters.

79. (A) Bipolar disorder counseling helps people with mania and sadness. This type of counselor helps people cope with mood fluctuations and maintain equilibrium.

80. (A) Body dysmorphia counseling focuses on assisting those who are suffering from body dysmorphic disorder (BDD), a condition marked by obsessive concerns with apparent flaws in one's appearance. Body dysmorphia counselors assist clients in exploring and challenging mistaken body image views, developing more accurate and constructive self-images, and reducing suffering connected to issues with body image.

81. (D) There is no agreement on the best way to modify tests for people with disabilities. The notion is novel, and more research is needed to evaluate the similarities that exist between the modified exam for disabilities and standardized tests in this field.

82. (C) Norms give significance to test scores and offer a basis for comparing scores to one another and to a norm.

83.	(C) Pastoral counseling will benefit the pious, pastoral client who believes the condition is a penalty for sin. A pastor with counseling training can assist the client reconcile religion and health.

84.	(B) Self-harm in eating disorder patients must be monitored. It can involve cutting, biting, and hair-pulling. Self-harming might increase as clients strive to control eating disorders.

85.	(D) Interventions can be implemented after the appraisal is over.

86.	(A) Assessing client strengths and resources include finding and comprehending the client's unique talents, competencies, and assets to help them recover and advance.

87.	(C) Rating compliance with limiting diets may be viewed as a punishment, especially if the client obtains low grades. It would be more efficient to provide positive feedback when the client performs well.

88.	(C) Treatment planning commonly includes steps like goal setting, identifying interventions, determining sessions, and reviewing and updating treatment plans.

89.	(B) The client must give informed consent and agree to the treatment plans and understand any risks that may arise.

90.	(D) Specific, measurable, and quantifiable goals allow objective progress measurement. Setting quantifiable goals helps counselors and clients measure progress, change interventions, and evaluate the treatment approach's efficacy.

91.	(A) Short-term goals allow counselors to monitor progress within a designated time frame.

92.	(C) Evidence-based treatment plans are well-written. The treatment plan's treatments and techniques have been proven to address the client's specific issues.

93.	(D) Circumstances and goals change during counseling. Counselors can keep the treatment plan pertinent, adaptable, and aligned with the client's needs and ambitions by reviewing and changing treatment goals and objectives.

94.	(C) Effective counseling requires cultural awareness and respect. Culturally sensitive treatment plans acknowledge and integrate the client's cultural background, principles, and preferences, improving the therapeutic partnership, client participation, and treatment outcomes.

95. (C) Counselors can improve treatment by tailoring it to the client's needs. This may involve adapting procedures, approaches, or strategies to the client's cultural background, cognitive stage, or goals, creating an individualized and client-centered treatment experience.

96. (C) Frameworks help counselors comprehend client concerns, choose suitable solutions, and plan treatment.

97. (D) Counselors can evaluate interventions, make revisions, and adjust treatment plans by regularly monitoring client progress. This process encourages responsiveness and maximizes success.

98. (C) Counselors may struggle to create comprehensive, evidence-based treatment plans without proper training or professional development.

99. (C) Active client involvement in treatment planning strengthens the therapeutic connection, empowers clients to participate in their treatment, and promotes collaboration and joint decision-making.

100. (C) Nonverbal gestures like eye contact are especially important for building trust, showing attention, and showing empathy.

101. (B) Empathic responding requires actively listening, understanding, and reflecting the client's ideas, emotions, and thoughts. Empathic counselors help clients feel heard, acknowledged, and understood.

102. (A) Counselors paraphrase clients' words to clarify meaning, reflect understanding, and assure accuracy.

103. (C) Open-ended inquiries allow clients to reflect, learn, and explore. They also encourage a collaborative, client-centered approach where clients actively shape counseling sessions.

104. (C) Counselors must actively listen to clients' communication cues with real interest and participation. It entails being present, eliminating distractions, and employing nonverbal indicators like eye contact and body language to show support.

105. (C) Reflecting on feelings helps clients gain understanding, self-awareness, and emotional healing during counseling.

106. (C) Summarizing captures a session's important points, topics, and key information.

107. (B) Preventing anxiety is the main goal when a client is approaching an impending panic attack. The best response is to ask if the client would feel better with an open door.

108. (C) This question only accepts "yes" or "no" answers about the client's emotional state. Closed-ended questions help acquire precise information, but they limit self-reflection.

109.   (D) Motivational interviewing encourages clients to modify detrimental behaviors. Counselors collaborate and empathize to understand the client's values, goals, and change ambivalence.

110.   (B) Compassion fatigue numbs the counselor to others' suffering. Repeated difficulties can cause it.

111.   (B) Empathy is shown in therapy through reflective listening. It entails actively listening to the client's nonverbal and verbal exchanges and then reflecting their thoughts back to them.

112.   (D) Counselors ask questions to help clients elaborate, provide perspective, and reflect on their concerns.

113.   (B) Silence lets clients think, feel, and reflect. Self-awareness, insight, and new viewpoints can result.

114.   (C) Active listening includes eye contact, nodding, appropriate facial expressions, and verbal affirmations (e.g., "I understand," "Go on"). These nonverbal and verbal clues show the client that the counselor is there, engaged, and listening.

115.   (A) Confrontation softly and respectfully questions the client's assumptions, inconsistencies, or disparities in thoughts, feelings, or behaviors. It raises awareness of patterns or ideas that may be hindering the client. Confrontation enables clients to examine new ideas, challenge their thinking, and evolve.

116.   (B) Reflecting feelings allows the counselor to look at the emotional content of a client's message and let them know they are being heard.

117.   (C) Scaling inquiries ask clients to rate their thoughts, feelings, and experiences on a 1–10 scale. Scaling questions help measure changes, discover patterns, and explore variables that may affect the client's motivation or progress.

118.   (C) A counselor who is actively listening will always look out for nonverbal cues and thought patterns in conversations.

119.   (B) Psychoeducation informs clients about their issues, symptoms, and therapy options.

120.   (A) Unconditional positive regard is the foundation of client-centered counseling. Carl Rogers advocated for warmth, empathy, and honesty, as well as unconditional acceptance without reserve.

121.   (C) Self-disclosure in counseling builds empathy and rapport. Self-disclosure allows the counselor to relate to the client and create trust.

122. (D) Advanced empathy involves reflecting on content and feelings. It entails accurately collecting and portraying the client's facts and emotions, showing a profound comprehension of their experience.

123. (A) Cognitive restructuring helps clients identify and correct their situation-related cognitive distortions.

124. (D) Donald Super's archway model illustrates various aspects that shape self-concept.

125. (C) Group pattern indicates group working and can vary, but if one individual dominates, it can affect the group as a whole.

126. (D) Analogies are metaphorical stories or metaphors used in therapy. It simplifies complex concepts and circumstances for clients.

127. (D) Solution-focused brief therapy seeks solutions. It explores the client's skills, resources, and goals and collaborates to achieve goals quickly.

128. (A) In 1884, James Lange propounded his Theory of Emotions, stating that physiological reactions come before the associated emotions.

129. (A) RET counselors confront irrational thoughts, provide clients with assignments to assist them quit irrational thinking and beneficial self-talk, and support positive thoughts, feelings, and actions.

130. (D) Working through resistance helps the client identify and overcome any resistance to change, advancing therapy.

131. (D) Counseling's behavioral activation aims to boost good behavior. It targets distress-causing and negative-emotion-maintaining behaviors to promote healthier and more adaptive ones.

132. (D) Summarizing entails helping the client examine different options.

133. (D) Normalization in counseling reduces isolation and abnormality by highlighting that their thoughts, feelings, and behaviors are common.

134. (D) Resource identification recognizes and uses the client's internal and external resources to promote well-being and change.

135. (D) Psychoanalytic therapy helps clients understand their unconscious motivations, childhood experiences, and how unresolved conflicts affect their ideas, feelings, and behaviors.

136. (A) Paraphrasing shows active listening and allows the counselor to express the client's views and experiences.

137. (D) Grounding strategies minimize anxiety and increase present-moment awareness.

138. (D) Problem-solving helps clients find realistic answers by developing and assessing strategies.

139. (D) Person-centered therapy aims to establish a safe and accepting environment. The therapeutic partnership, unconditional positive regard, and empathetic understanding encourage self-exploration and personal progress.

140. (B) These terms were coined by Carl Jung.

141. (D) Reframing in therapy provides new viewpoints and interpretations. It entails helping clients obtain fresh perspectives and modify their thinking.

142. (D) Addressing ambivalence recognizes that clients may have conflicting emotions about making changes and assists them in navigating and resolving their uncertainties.

143. (D) Using reinforcement, modeling, and behavior modification, behavioral therapy identifies and changes behaviors that cause discomfort or harm the client.

144. (C) Summarizing consolidates material, highlights vital aspects, and ensures counselor-client clarity.

145. (D) Relaxation techniques reduce anxiety, quiet the mind and body, and teach self-soothing and emotional control.

146. (D) Cognitive restructuring challenges and reframes problematic thoughts and beliefs to promote accurate, positive thinking that encourages emotional well-being and adaptive behaviors.

147. (D) Motivational interviewing encourages transformation. This collaborative, client-centered approach helps clients explore and address their ambivalence about change, motivating them to make beneficial behavioral adjustments.

148. (C) Understanding and sharing the client's emotions, viewpoints, and experiences creates a helpful and validating therapeutic partnership.

149. (D) Being honest and open in therapy builds trust and rapport with clients.

150. (D) Unconditional positive regard involves accepting and valuing clients as persons without judgment or constraints, creating a secure and non-judgmental space.

151. (B) Counseling requires honesty and congruence. Consistency, transparency, and honesty are key. Congruence increases trust and authenticity in therapy.

152. (C) Developmental needs form the very core of the counseling profession.

153. (A) A bond of confidence along with mutual understanding is exemplified by therapeutic alliance.

154. (B) Congruence means putting aside personal preconceptions and prejudices and allowing clients to openly express themselves.
155. (D) Recognizing and appreciating clients' cultures and minimizing any negative impact on the counseling process is cultural competence.
156. (A) Respect implies valuing clients and their freedoms. It involves acknowledging their decisions and actively involving them in counseling.
157. (D) Bandura believed that self-efficacy is a must for therapy to be successful.
158. (C) Hypnosis is a state of deep relaxation. It leads to the mind becoming more open to guidance.
159. (B) Cause and effect are only determinable by experiments.
160. (D) Boundaries necessitate client privacy and confidentiality. They include protecting client confidentiality and professional limits throughout counseling.

Bonus Fifty

Before we conclude, here are fifty more questions and answers on different NCE core areas, just so you have more practice going into the exam!

1. A career counselor may give their clients which of these tests in following Holland's theories of career choice?

   A. SCII
   B. MMPI
   C. KOIS
   D. SDS

2. The father of sociology is:

   A. Sigmund Freud
   B. Emile Durkheim
   C. Alfred Binet
   D. Eric Berne

3. What information must be gathered when planning a learning experience for a group of homeless individuals with substance abuse issues?

   A. Community aids
   B. Inpatient care
   C. Drugs to treat substance abuse disorder
   D. Individual commitment

4. When was the first psychosocial laboratory established?

   A. 1879
   B. 1890
   C. 1913 1927

5. Who began using psychoanalysis to treat mental illness in 1890?

   A. Wilhelm Wundt

    B. Jesse Davis
    C. Sigmund Freud
    D. Frank Parsons

6. In which year did Jesse Davis start working as a professional counselor at Detroit High School?

    A. 1879
    B. 1898
    C. 1913
    D. 1954

7. Which book, published in 1908, exposed conditions within mental health institutions?

    A. A Mind That Found Itself
    B. Choosing A Vocation
    C. Counseling And Psychotherapy
    D. The Counselor in a Changing World

8. Who directed the Vocation Bureau based in Boston in 1908?

    A. Wilhelm Wundt
    B. Jesse Davis
    C. Sigmund Freud
    D. Frank Parsons

9. What year marked the foundation of the National Vocational Guidance Association, the first counseling association?

    A. 1898
    B. 1913
    C. 1942
    D. 1951

10. In 1927, which career assessment tool was published by E. K. Strong?

    A. A Mind That Found Itself
    B. The Strong-Vocational Interest Blank
    C. How To Counsel Students
    D. The Counselor in a Changing World

11. In what year was the American Personnel and Guidance Association established?

    A. 1879
    B. 1913
    C. 1951
    D. 1981

12. When did the American Association for Counseling and Development (AACD) become the American Counseling Association (ACA)?

    A. 1927
    B. 1954
    C. 1976
    D. 992

13. When did California pass legislation for counselor licensure?

    A. 1981
    B. 1990
    C. 2000s
    D. 2010

14. Which event in 2010 led to the establishment of the Disaster Mental Health program category?

    A. National convention by the American Counseling Association (ACA)
    B. Revisions of the CACREP
    C. American Association of State Counseling Boards (AASCB) involvement
    D. ACA guidelines on distance counseling

15. What factors contribute to the dynamic scope of counseling practice?

    A. Changing state laws and influence from other professions
    B. The establishment of the Disaster Mental Health program
    C. The role of the American Association of State Counseling Boards (AASCB)
    D. The integration of advocacy competencies

16. Which organization helps licensed counselors transition between different states?

    A. American Counseling Association (ACA)
    B. American Association of State Counseling Boards (AASCB)
    C. The CACREP
    D. American Group Psychotherapy Association (AGPA)

17. What does social justice in counseling aim to promote?

    A. Wellness and technology
    B. Spirituality and multiculturalism
    C. Fairness, justice, and a greater balance of power and resources
    D. Evidence-based methods and coalitions

18. Why is an awareness of the relationship between the functions of our bodies and mental behavior important for counselors?

    A. To protect client confidentiality and autonomy
    B. To ensure cognizance of brain and biological functions for diagnoses and counseling
    C. To advocate for constructive changes in laws and policies
    D. To use technology and social media for advocacy messages

19. Which guidelines provide ethical standards for distance counseling?

    A. Advocacy Competencies by the ACA
    B. Code of Ethics by the ACA
    C. Disaster Mental Health program guidelines

D. Competencies for Client/Student Empowerment

20. Which advocacy competency focuses on educating advocacy activities and supporting successful policies and programs?

    A. Advocating for policies promoting fairness, justice, and well-being
    B. Building coalitions and alliances with various stakeholders
    C. Employing evidence-based methods
    D. Evaluating the effectiveness of lobbying activities

21. What is the goal of empowerment counselor competencies?

    A. System change interventions and empowerment strategy implementation
    B. Identifying external barriers that could impact development
    C. Self-advocacy and action plan development
    D. Carrying out action plans and promoting self-care

22. Which competency involves recognizing signs indicating individual behaviors and concerns reflect responses to oppression?

    A. Identifying resources and strengths of students and clients
    B. Identifying different political, economic, social, and cultural factors impacting clients and students
    C. Recognizing signs of oppression-related responses
    D. Assisting clients and students in carrying out action plans

23. How can counselors help clients and students in self-advocacy?

    A. Train clients and students to self-advocate
    B. Develop action plans for self-advocacy
    C. Assist in carrying out action plans
    D. All of the above

24. In how many US states and the District of Columbia is physician-assisted suicide allowed?

    A. 5

B. 8

C. 10

D. 12

25. Which of the following states does NOT allow physician-assisted suicide?

A. Montana

B. California

C. New Jersey

D. Maine

26. What are the eligibility criteria for physician-assisted suicide?

A. Having a terminal condition and a life expectancy of six months or fewer

B. Being over 65 years old

C. Being diagnosed with a mental illness

D. Requesting it voluntarily

27. What is the purpose of a disclosure and informed consent statement in counseling?

A. To protect client privacy and confidentiality

B. To inform clients about potential dangers and benefits of counseling

C. To clarify the counselor-client roles and duties

D. All of the above

28. Why is a disclosure and informed consent statement important in therapy?

A. It ensures that clients have all the necessary information about counseling

B. It allows clients to make an informed decision regarding participation

C. It builds trust and clarity between the counselor and the client

D. All of the above

29. In what situations can counselors be held legally responsible and sued?

A. Causing mental distress to clients

   B. Engaging in sexual harassment or misconduct

   C. Being negligent in providing professional services

   D. All of the above

30. What conditions that must be met for a successful malpractice claim against a counselor?

   A. Establishing a professional relationship, breach of duty, client suffering harm, and harm caused by breach of duty

   B. Client consent, proper documentation, adherence to treatment plans, and avoidance of false claims

   C. Privacy protection, parental access to education records, equal chances for women in sports, and mental health coverage

   D. Compliance with insurance company requirements, maintaining a provider list status, cost reduction, and proper diagnosis

31. What is the purpose of the Family Educational Rights and Privacy Act (FERPA)?

   A. To protect individual privacy

   B. To provide equal chances for women in sports

   C. To regulate managed health care policies

   D. To establish guidelines for disclosure and informed consent in counseling

32. What is the main goal of Title IX of the educational amendments?

   A. To ban sex discrimination in schools, academics, and athletics

   B. To protect client confidentiality in counseling

   C. To promote managed health care policies

   D. To provide equal access to education records

33. Which is NOT a component of social and cultural diversity?

   A. Multicultural and pluralistic trends

   B. Cultural identity

   C. Racial identity models

D. Communication patterns

34. What does cultural encapsulation refer to?

    A. Treating and evaluating from a dominant culture point of view
    B. Embracing cultural diversity in counseling
    C. Integrating cultural identities in the counseling process
    D. Understanding the impact of cultural factors on identity development

35. What does multicultural counseling involve?

    A. Recognizing and appreciating diversity
    B. Eliminating prejudices and biases
    C. Tailoring counseling interventions to cultural contexts
    D. All of the above

36. What is cultural identity?

    A. Belonging and attachment to a particular cultural group or community
    B. The integration of cultural identities with the counseling process
    C. The elimination of biases and discrimination in counseling
    D. The understanding of clients' different values and beliefs

37. Who developed the first racial identity model?

    A. William Cross Jr.
    B. C. Gilbert Wrenn
    C. Carl Rogers
    D. Sigmund Freud

38. What are the three components of the Tripartite model of multicultural counseling?

    A. Knowledge, skills, and awareness
    B. Beliefs, attitudes, and values
    C. Culture, language, and customs
    D. Individual, couple, and group strategies

39. What does the term "etic" refer to?

    A. Viewing clients from a universal point of view
    B. Viewing situations from the cultural perspective of a client
    C. Using non-verbal cues in communication
    D. Studying the perception and use of time in communication

40. What does proxemics refer to?

    A. The study of body movements and facial expressions
    B. The perception and use of time in communication
    C. The different zones of personal physical distance
    D. The process of adjusting to a new culture

41. What does the assimilation model of acculturation involve?

    A. Giving up one's cultural identity to conform to the dominant culture
    B. Separating from the dominant culture and maintaining one's own culture
    C. Identifying with one's own and other cultures
    D. Rejecting the cultural customs and values of both one's own and the dominant cultures

42. Classical conditioning involves the association between a _____ and an _____ to elicit a response.

    A. Conditioned stimulus; unconditioned stimulus
    B. Neutral stimulus; conditioned response
    C. Reinforcement; punishment
    D. Positive consequence; negative consequence

43. Operant conditioning focuses on how behaviors are influenced by their _____.

    A. Consequences
    B. Stimuli
    C. Associations

D. Observations

44. Social learning theory emphasizes the importance of _____ in shaping behavior and attitudes.

   A. Reinforcement
   B. Observation
   C. Punishment
   D. Conditioning

45. The Dollard and Miller approach highlights the role of _____ in shaping behavior.

   A. Drives
   B. Cues
   C. Reinforcement
   D. Observation

46. Lev Vygotsky's cognitive development theory emphasizes the role of _____ in shaping cognitive development.

   A. Genetic factors
   B. Environmental experiences
   C. Social interactions
   D. All of the above

47. Positive transference in therapy refers to the client projecting _____ feelings onto the therapist.

   A. Negative
   B. Neutral
   C. Positive
   D. Unresolved

48. Client resistance in counseling can manifest as _____.

   A. Trust and openness
   B. Minimization of issues

C. Collaborative exploration

D. Rapport and safe environment

49. The integrative ACT intervention model combines acceptance, mindfulness, and clarifying _____.

A. Personal values

B. Cognitive defusion

C. Committed action

D. Self-as-context

50. Which of the following test items requires respondents to choose from two or more specific response options without allowing open-ended answers?

A. Dichotomous items

B. Difficulty index

C. External validity

D. Forced choice items

Answer Key

Q.	1	2	3	4	5	6	7	8	9	10
A.	D	B	A	A	C	B	A	D	B	B

Q.	11	12	13	14	15	16	17	18	19	20
A.	C	D	D	A	A	B	C	B	B	C

Q.	21	22	23	24	25	26	27	28	29	30
A.	A	C	D	C	D	A	D	D	D	A

Q.	31	32	33	34	35	36	37	38	39	40
A.	A	A	C	A	D	A	A	A	A	C

Q.	41	42	43	44	45	46	47	48	49	50
A.	A	A	A	B	C	D	C	B	A	D

Free Video Offer!

Thank you for purchasing from Hanley Test Preparation! We're honored to help you prepare for your exam. To show our appreciation, we're offering an Exclusive Test Tips Video.

This video includes multiple strategies that will make you successful on your big exam.

All we ask is that you email us your feedback and describe your experience with our product. Amazing, awful, or just so-so. We want to hear what you have to say!

To get your FREE VIDEO, just send us an email at bonusvideo@hanleytestprep.com with **Free Video** in the subject line and the following information in the body of the email:

- The name of the product you purchased
- Your product rating on a scale of 1-5, with 5 being the highest rating.
- Your feedback about the product.

If you have any questions or concerns, please don't hesitate to contact us at support@hanleytestprep.com

Thanks again!

Conclusion

We have now reached the end of this book. Before you get busy with your preparations, here are some parting words. Remember, the best performers are those who make plans. A little thing I like to do is take a pretest before I sit down to make a study plan. This is because, as someone who's going to appear for a licensing exam, chances are you are already familiar with a lot of the content. Doing this pretest will help you identify your natural strengths and weaknesses, which will, in turn, be helpful when preparing your schedule and timetable.

Prepare for the various sections of the NCE test, keeping in mind that certain curriculum areas will have a much larger number of questions than others. While there are 11 questions devoted to the topic of Social and Cultural Foundations, there are 36 questions dedicated to Helping Relationships. Your strategy should always account for dividing time in a way that'll help you get through each section with minimum hassle.

If you finished school a while back and there is a gap, I recommend setting up a study plan that will last for two months. I would study a new topic each week, remembering that, in certain weeks, more time would be needed than others due to unfamiliarity with the subject or a higher concentration of questions from that topic on the test.

Beginning with the second week, go back and review what you studied each earlier week so you don't forget the essentials. Leave important anecdotes and mark the sections that feel tricky. The more you review, the more you'll remember.

Schedule your study hours before you sit down. A lot of preparatory materials will ask that you begin studying in the morning, but I've found that some of us are more content to study and work at night because we feel more alert once the world is quiet. I would emphasize choosing a time that feels most right for you, so long as you are still getting eight hours of sleep. DO NOT compromise on rest.

Don't burden yourself with excessive materials and a truckload of information from a hundred different resources. This just makes the process frustrating and can be very immobilizing. Instead, choose two to three important resources to pace yourself.

The NCE cutoff has never been higher than 65%. This means getting 104 marks out of 160. It sounds very hard at first, but this is a very reasonable cutoff, which means that the NCE is a very doable exam. All you need is to prepare well and give it your best shot. If you can, try to know if your state will convert the NCE cutoff to a higher percentage before calling it a pass, and prepare your mindset accordingly.

Engage actively. Take notes, underline relevant passages, and create brief summaries to help you retain information. Make an effort to use what you're learning in practical ways.

View the exam preparation stage as something you are doing to get even better as a professional. It isn't something you need to do as an unpleasant formality. Rather, it exists so you become better equipped to make others do better in life. That is the overarching purpose of the NCE.

Go into the process with an open mind and heart, and you will surely do well! All the best with your preparations. I hope you enjoyed following along, and if you did, don't forget to leave a review on Amazon!

References

American Counseling Association. (2019). *ACA Milestones*. Counseling. org. https://www.counseling.org/about-us/about-aca/our-history/aca-milestones

CACREP. (2016). *2016 CACREP Standards | CACREP*. Cacrep.org. https://www.cacrep.org/for-programs/2016-cacrep-standards/

CDC. (2021, April 6). *Facts about Down Syndrome | CDC*. Centers for Disease Control and Prevention. https://www.cdc.gov/ncbddd/birthdefects/downsyndrome.html#

Chegg. (n.d.). *NCE - Counseling and Helping Relationships, Group Dynamics Flashcards | Chegg.com*. Www.chegg.com. Retrieved June 8, 2023, from https://www.chegg.com/flashcards/nce-counseling-and-helping-relationships-group-dynamics-461827de-0e61-4a55-9c9b-b34c-2d73e507/deck

Cherry, K. (2019, November 27). *How and When Confidential Information Can Be Disclosed in Therapy*. Verywell Mind. https://www.verywellmind.com/what-is-duty-to-warn-2795096

Cherry, K. (2022, December 16). *The 4 Stages of Cognitive Development*. Verywell Mind; Dotdash Meredith. https://www.verywellmind.com/piagets-stages-of-cognitive-development-2795457

Cherry, K. (2023, February 23). *How Classical Conditioning works: an Overview with Examples*. Verywell Mind. https://www.verywellmind.com/classical-conditioning-2794859

CNN Library. (2020, June 11). *Physician-Assisted Suicide Fast Facts*. CNN; CNN. https://www.cnn.com/2014/11/26/us/physician-assisted-suicide-fast-facts/index.html

COU 522 Human Growth and Development NCE review. (n.d.). Studylib. net. Retrieved June 3, 2023, from https://studylib.net/doc/5477060/cou-522-human-growth-and-development-nce-review

Erford, B. T., Hays, D. G., & Crockett, S. A. (2020). *Mastering the National Counselor Examination and the Counselor Preparation Comprehensive Examination*. Pearson Education, Inc.

Fitzgibbons, L. (2019, December). *Social Learning Theory*. WhatIs. com. https://www.techtarget.com/whatis/definition/social-learning-theory#:~:text=Social%20learning%20theory%20is%20the

Ford, J. D., Grasso, D. J., Elhai, J. D., & Courtois, C. A. (2015). Social, cultural, and other diversity issues in the traumatic stress field. *Posttraumatic Stress Disorder*, 503–546. https://doi.org/10.1016/B978-0-12-801288-8.00011-X

Genetic Alliance, & District of Columbia Department of Health. (2010, February 17). *Single-Gene Disorders*. Nih.gov; Genetic Alliance. https://www.ncbi.nlm.nih.gov/books/NBK132154/

Granich, S. (2014, November 16). *Duty to Warn, Duty to Protect*. SocialWorker. com. https://www.socialworker.com/feature-articles/ethics-articles/Duty_to_Warn%2C_Duty_to_Protect/

Hirsch, L. (2018). *Brain and Nervous System (for Teens)*. Kidshealth.org. https://kidshealth.org/en/teens/brain-nervous-system.html

How Long Does It Take to Become a Licensed Counselor? (n.d.). CORP-MAC0 (OCP). https://onlinecounselingprograms.com/become-a-counselor/how-long-does-it-take/

Litchfield, K. A., & Lambert, M. C. (2011). *Nativist Theory* (S. Goldstein & J. A. Naglieri, Eds.). Springer Link; Springer US. https://link.springer.com/10.1007%2F978-0-387-79061-9_1911

Lumen. (n.d.). *The Humanistic Perspective | Lifespan Development*. Courses.lumenlearning.com. https://courses.lumenlearning.com/wm-lifespandevelopment/chapter/the-humanistic-perspective/

Macdonald, A. (2011). *Solution-Focused Therapy: Theory, Research & Practice*. SAGE Knowledge; SAGE Publications Ltd. https://sk.sagepub.com/books/solution-focused-therapy-2e/n6.xml

Mcleod, S. (2019, July 18). *Psychosexual Stages*. Simplypsychology.org; Simply Psychology. https://www.simplypsychology.org/psychosexual.html

Mcleod, S. (2023). *Vygotsky's Sociocultural Theory of Cognitive Development*. Simply Psychology. https://www.simplypsychology.org/vygotsky.html

MedicineNet. (2019, December 17). *Nature vs. Nurture Theory Explained: Effects on Genes and Intelligence*. MedicineNet. https://www.medicinenet.com/nature_vs_nurture_theory_genes_or_environment/article.htm

Medline Plus. (2020, September 17). *What is a gene mutation and how do mutations occur?: MedlinePlus Genetics*. Medlineplus.gov. https://medlineplus.gov/genetics/understanding/mutationsanddisorders/genemutation/

Medline Plus. (2021, May 14). *What are complex or multifactorial disorders?: MedlinePlus Genetics*. Medlineplus.gov. https://medlineplus.gov/genetics/understanding/mutationsanddisorders/complexdisorders/

Mometrix Exam Secrets Test Prep Team, & Mometrix Media Llc. (2018). *NCE : flashcard study system*. Mometrix Media Llc.

National Counselor Exam Study Guide Team. (2016). *NCE study guide*. Test Prep Books.

National Counselor Examination (NCE) Handbook as Part of the National Certified Counselor (NCC) Application. (2023). https://nbcc.org/Assets/Exam/Handbooks/NCE.pdf

National Institute of Neurological Disorders and Stroke. (2022, November 14). *Brain Basics: The Life and Death of a Neuron | National Institute of Neurological Disorders and Stroke.* Www.ninds.nih.gov. https://www.ninds.nih.gov/health-information/public-education/brain-basics/brain-basics-life-and-death-neuron

NCE exam preparation secrets : NCE study guide for the National Counselor Exam. (2021). Mometrix Media LLC.

NCE STUDY NOTES – Group Therapy | PDF | Group Psychotherapy | Psychotherapy. (n.d.). Scribd. Retrieved June 8, 2023, from https://www.scribd.com/document/518419512/NCE-STUDY-NOTES-Group-Therapy

Nguyen, K. V. (2019, March 25). *Privileged Communication vs Confidentiality In Counseling.* 8x8. https://www.8x8.com/blog/privileged-communication-vs-confidentiality-counseling

Niwlikar, B. (2021, June 12). *Dollard and Miller Stimulus Response Theory of Personality.* Careershodh. https://www.careershodh.com/dollard-and-miller-stimulus-response-theory-of-personality/

Puderbaugh, M., & Emmady, P. D. (2022, May 8). *Neuroplasticity.* PubMed; StatPearls Publishing. https://www.ncbi.nlm.nih.gov/books/NBK557811/

RajMohan, V., & Mohandas, E. (2007). The limbic system. *Indian Journal of Psychiatry, 49*(2), 132–139. https://doi.org/10.4103/0019-5545.33264

Ratts, M. J., Toporek, R. L., & Lewis, J. A. (2010). *ACA Advocacy Competencies: A Social Justice Framework for Counselors.*

Roshan Patel, & Sandeep Sharma. (2019, September 11). *Credentialing.* Nih.gov; StatPearls Publishing. https://www.ncbi.nlm.nih.gov/books/NBK519504/

Schwartz, B. (2017, October 27). *Three Main Reasons Clinicians Fail Their Clients Pt. 1*. New Harbinger Publications, Inc. https://www.newharbinger.com/blog/professional/three-main-reasons-clinicians-fail-their-clients-pt-1/

Social and Cultural Foundations Questions- Rosenthal 1-16 | National Counselor's Exam (NCE)Preparation. (2021, April 24). Blogs.depaul.edu. https://blogs.depaul.edu/coe-academic-success-center/2021/04/24/social-and-cultural-foundations-questions-rosenthal-1-16/

Staddon, J. E. R., & Cerutti, D. T. (2002). Operant conditioning. *Annual Review of Psychology, 54*(1), 115–144. https://doi.org/10.1146/annurev.psych.54.101601.145124

The Myers-Briggs Company. (2019). *Strong Interest Inventory® | Career test*. Themyersbriggs.com. https://www.themyersbriggs.com/en-US/Products-and-Services/Strong

The University of Queensland. (2018, July 17). *Lobes of the brain*. Queensland Brain Institute. https://qbi.uq.edu.au/brain/brain-anatomy/lobes-brain

Vandergriendt, C. (2022). *What Is a Neuron? Function, Parts, Structure, Types, and More*. Healthline. https://www.healthline.com/health/neurons

Walinga, J. (2014, October 17). *2.4 Humanist, Cognitive, and Evolutionary Psychology*. Opentextbc.ca; BCcampus. https://opentextbc.ca/introductiontopsychology/chapter/2-4-humanist-cognitive-and-evolutionary-psychology/

Additional Quizlets and Factsheets for Information

http://spectrum.troy.edu/mmatise/CompsPreparationProgram/8.%20
Professional%20Orientation%20and%20Ethical%20Practice%20Comps%20
Reivew.pdf

https://quizlet.com/216744709/nce-assessments-and-testing-flash-cards/

https://quizlet.com/507672975/nce-group-counseling-group-work-study-
questions-flash-cards/

https://quizlet.com/6138467/nce-exam-lifestyle-and-career-development-
flash-cards/

Made in United States
North Haven, CT
18 November 2023

44225633R00120